# Money Matters for

Adapted from materials by
# LARRY BURKETT
### with *Marnie Wooding*

*Illustrated by **Chris Kielesinski***

MOODY PRESS
CHICAGO

**Larry Burkett's Money Matters for Kids™**
Executive Producer: *Allen Burkett*

**For Lightwave**
Managing Editor: *Elaine Osborne*
Project Assistant: *Ed Strauss*
Text Director: *K. Christie Bowler*
Art Director: *Terry VanRoon*
Illustration Inking: *Ken Save*
Desktop Publishing: *Randy Christie*

ISBN: 0-8024-4636-1

5 7 9 10 8 6 4

*Printed in the United States of America*

# Contents

# CHAPTER 1

# Stewardship

# #1—Stewardship Matters

# The Spin on Stewardship

Does money matter to you? It should. You use it almost every day of your life. Search your pockets—find some loose change? Look at it carefully. Do you see the words "In God We Trust"? That is the heart of money matters. God and our use of money shouldn't be separated. God has His own spin on the way we should view both ourselves and our finances. To understand that spin let's find out a little more about a thing called stewardship.

There are stewards on airplanes, boats, and even in some hotels. The Bible talks about stewards—Joseph, Mephibosheth, and the kings all had them. A steward is a manager. In Luke 12, Jesus asks, *"Who then is the faithful and wise manager?"* What's the answer to that question? Not sure? Well then, you've come to the right place. Stewardship is what this book is all about. The most important thing to remember about money is that what we do with it is merely an outside indicator of what's going on inside of us.

It's really true—we are all stewards, no matter what our age or ability. What is a steward, anyway? Someone who takes care of, or manages, things that belong to someone else. You don't think you fall into that category? Psalm 24:1 says, *"The earth is the Lord's and everything in it, the world, and all who live in it."* If you are a Christian, then you understand that you belong to God—you are His child. If you don't know that, then here's the first step in the process: Jesus died for you. He paid the price for your sin, and He offers you eternal life with Him—if you will just accept His gift and ask Him to forgive you. That's the beginning of a new you and a new life. So, you know that you belong to God. "But," you ask, "what's this about all my stuff belonging to Him? I paid for it!" *Everything* belongs to Him! Remember Psalm 24:1?

# The Universal Owner

Let's get another take on *everything*. Go around and gather up all the brilliant scientists, inventors, and other "brains" from around the world. All that collected brainpower may know a whole lot about many things, but they can't know everything. The only One who knows absolutely everything about everything, from the supergalaxies in space to the microscopic atoms that make up this page, is God. *"He determines the number of the stars and calls them each by name. Great is our Lord and mighty in power; his understanding has no limit"* (Psalm 147:4–5).

OK, what about the fact that God owns everything, too? Yes, even the supergalaxies and the microscopic atoms. Our entire world is one big lifetime gift to us from God. He is letting us look after *His* things. God has given us everything we need, from our breath to the house we live in. It is our job to take care of the things God has given us, from the people we love to the little things we use every day to make our lives easier. They are all God's gifts, whether they seem important or not.

We need to be faithful stewards with things like family, friends, church, careers, talents, and abilities. God's gifts come in all shapes and sizes. Being a good steward can, at first, sound overwhelming. Relax! God teaches and helps us in a way that is everything but overwhelming. God set up this whole system of stewardship, not to make it harder on us, but better for us.

God has given us things, abilities, and talents that help us serve others, not just ourselves. Did you know that the people in our own lives—parents, teachers, friends, ministers and bosses—are God's gifts to us? When we manage the things God has given us according to His plan, our lives are better and we are a benefit to all the people God has put around us.

Does it seem like there is a galaxy of things we have to do to be better stewards? Where can we start? Well, just like a trek in space, there are points to guide our way. How to handle our attitudes and make decisions about our careers, our money, and our future are points that may need a little exploration. Do these parts of your life seem a little alien? Don't worry, this book will help you learn how to get through your life trek at warp speed—guided by God's communication devices—the Bible, prayer, and wise counsel. So let's take a look at these ideas. After we finish, money matters might not seem as mysterious as those black holes in space!

# #2—The Character of God

# The List

"Does God really care what I do with my career, my money, my future? What difference do these decisions make to Him?" Since God made you in His image, what you do matters a lot to Him. Remember the Ten Commandments? God gave us those commandments as a standard of living that would rightly reflect His character. God alone is holy, therefore we should not worship anyone or anything else—including sports, big-name entertainers, fame, or fortune! You want to know how to tell what you are worshiping? Well, take a look at the number one priority in your life—what do you spend the most time thinking about or most of your money on? Is it football, cheerleading, computers, band, drama club, youth group? Why are those things important to you? Is it to look good, to become popular, or just because it's what everyone else is doing? Watch out! Your worship may not be focused on God. It's not *what* you're doing that's the problem . . . it's *why*.

God has given you special abilities, talents, and gifts that make up who you are and what you enjoy doing. These things are all part of the plan He has for your life. And the plan He has for you goes together with the plan He has for your family. That goes with the plan for your church, which goes with the plan for your community, your country, and your world. All these go together to make up His plan for eternity. When our worship is focused on God, we are listening to His leading, and following His plan to a life that is an adventure. When our families, our churches, our communities, our countries, our world join in—that is *life* God's way! And that is why God wants us to worship Him alone—only *He* has all the answers to life's questions.

# Why The List?

Well, on with the other commandments. God wants us to choose our words carefully and use His name properly because He is who He is; He never changes. He wants us to take time to rest and think about His creativity in our lives so that we don't get so busy that we forget His work in and around us. Part of following the plan is listening to and respecting the people that care for us and work with us—beginning with our parents. God is responsible for those over us and He wants us to show our trust in His plan. The commandments tell us the big things like don't take another's life because God is life. But they also tell about the smaller, but equally important, everyday things like being faithful in our relationships, pure in our thoughts, having integrity, and being truthful. All because God is faithful to us. He is holy and He is true. God wants us to understand that wrong attitudes and actions are not in His plan for us. Being dishonest can damage the reputation of someone God loves and wanting the things God has given someone else can harm both ourselves and our relationships. When we bring wrong attitudes, reactions, and actions into our lives they block both our focus on God and the plan He has for us.

You see, you have a choice about what you bring into your life and your relationship with God. God has given you His checklist on what you need. If you have attitudes and actions that don't match up to God's Word you also have the choice about taking them out of your life. God can help you clean house and replace those old ways with better ways. The direction you go is completely up to you.

Before you make that choice let's think about why we should truly reflect God. The Bible says that God is love. Everything God does is absolutely unselfish and giving. That sounds pretty awesome. When someone loves you, don't they usually want the best for you? This is absolutely the case with God. He wants the best for you, and He alone knows absolutely what is best for you. God's way is the way we should choose because His way naturally matches the way He created the world. Creation is the way it is because God is the way He is. When we act, show, and do the things that reflect God's heart, we are doing things the right way. His way equals a better life.

Think of God's way of doing things as an instruction guide to using His gifts. We wouldn't try to put together a new computer system or a new *anything* without reading the instructions first, right? Why would we try to put our own lives together without instructions? The Bible is His instruction book on how to put our lives together according to His will. You can count on it.

# #3—Trusting God

# Trust in Action

In the movies, the hero always seems to be able to come out of amazing, dangerous adventures all by himself. One man or woman alone against the world. Well, that's how it is in the movies. Real life is different. In real life we don't have to go it alone. We can trust God to be with us all the time. We may not always be aware of His support and guidance in our lives, but it's there. Sometimes it is tempting to just do things our way. Stop! Trusting God also means having the patience to wait for His advice.

# Trust, the Lifeline

Way back on April 11, 1970, the spacecraft Apollo 13 was launched. Three astronauts were sent into space. Their mission was to land on the moon. Unfortunately, due to a ruptured oxygen tank, the crew was faced with extremely serious and life-threatening difficulties. Their mission to the moon was aborted, and the struggle to return them safely to Earth began. They endured days of uncertainty while they waited for the experts on Earth to make plans for them. It was a pretty tense situation all around. Finally, Apollo 13 was able to splash down in the South Pacific on April 17. Even though the Apollo crew were true life superheroes, they didn't return safely all on their own. Remember, this is real life, not the movies. The crew had to rely on the many dedicated specialists back at mission control.

How does this little bit of space history relate to trust? On their own abilities, the crew would never have returned safely. They could have tried to handle the situation alone and done things their way. After all, mission control was thousands of miles away. Instead, the three astronauts put their trust in the professional men and women back on Earth. They listened and did what mission control advised them to do. The crew understood that the people back home had the knowledge to help them and wanted to do the best for them.

Sometimes it may feel like God is a million miles away, or that He isn't there for you. It's hard to be patient and wait for His messages. But, like the crew out in space, you have to trust that God is your own personal mission control. If you do things God's way, follow His instruction manual, and trust Him to take care of you, your life will work out better.

# Stay in Touch

The Apollo 13 spacecraft was constantly being monitored by Earth. Everything that went on in that ship, mission control knew about—sometimes even before it happened. Guess what? God's the ultimate mission control. Nothing happens in our lives that He doesn't know about. We need and want "God contact" in our lives! We get our "God contact" through prayer and reading His instruction manual. We can talk to God about everything in our lives, the great things and the problems. So stop and spend some quiet time getting His instructions and picking up on His signals. Without them, we could drift through our lives like a ship lost in space.

You don't have to do anything special or be a heroic astronaut to earn God's love. You just have to be you. *"May the God of hope fill you with all joy and peace as you trust in him, so that you may overflow with hope by the power of the Holy Spirit"* (Romans 15:13). The story of the Apollo 13 crew is one of challenge and victory. No doubt about it. When we do things God's way, the end of the story is even better. When we put our lives and our future in God's hands we know everything is complete and under control. Remember, God knows everything, is everywhere, and can do anything! God has a mission to teach us His ways and take care of us. When we learn to listen to God we get joy, peace, and hope. When we trust God, we are entering a fail-safe zone. God doesn't fail us and He keeps us safe. You can take that back to Earth!

# #4—You Want Me to Be a Steward of What?

# The Steward's List

We all have different things God has given us to be stewards of, but there are some basic categories that apply to everyone. Let's take a look at seven of them.

## Our Relationship with God

## Our Relationship with Others

## Who We Are

## What We Choose

## What We Do With Our Time

## What We Own

## What We Are Able to Do

# Our Relationship with God

When you play a one-on-one sport like tennis, all your concentration is focused on the other player. You watch every move and gesture he makes. Our relationship with God should be that focused. It takes concentration, determination, and commitment. God should be our number one love. We should keep not only our eyes on Him, but our hearts as well.

How do we get a close relationship with God? Just like in sports, we've got to put in the training and the playing time. Training comes when we take time and commitment to pray and read the Bible. When we pray, we need to tell God our private thoughts and feelings. It's often during those one-on-one quiet times that God puts His wisdom and direction in our thoughts. Just like we can't become great athletes overnight, it also takes time and energy to grow in our walk with God. Just take one day at a time. The playing time is actually going out and doing what we learn. Ask God to help you discipline yourself to spend more time with Him.

# Our Relationship with Others

Hello . . . anybody out there? It would be a pretty lonely universe if you were the only one in it. God created us to be with others. He wants us to have family, friends, and coworkers. We should care for and love the people in our lives in the same unselfish way that God does.

The world is full of people that think only of themselves or what people can do for them. God really doesn't want us to use people. He wants us to be *useful*. In our relationships with others, we should think about what we can do for them. Jesus put our salvation before His own life. That's the kind of relationship our Lord has with us. What kind of relationship do you have with others? Is it selfish or selfless? Show the people in your life how much you care by thinking about their needs before your own. Be a good steward of your relationships by being loving, generous, forgiving, and supportive—important starting points to building lifelong friendships. Being a good steward of relationships means trusting God that His way to treat others is the best way for our lives and theirs.

# Who We Are

Go look in the mirror and come back. Well? What did you see? Yourself, right? And? Did you like what you saw? God sees us for exactly who we are, and He loves what He sees because He made each of us special. God's Word helps show us who we are, how we should treat ourselves, and how we can keep growing to be what God wants us to be. It's all part of God's mirror, and it will tell us the truth about ourselves. *"Anyone who listens to the word but does not do what it says is like a man who looks at his face in a mirror and, after looking at himself, goes away and immediately forgets what he looks like. But the man who looks intently into the perfect law that gives freedom, and continues to do this, not forgetting what he has heard, but doing it— he will be blessed in what he does"* (James 1:23–25). Sometimes we keep checking in the world's mirror—that's like looking in a carnival mirror. Things get distorted because the world is giving us wrong life goals and ideas that are out of sync with God's will and plan for us.

God made you, and like the galaxies in space, you are awesome. *"I praise you because I am fearfully and wonderfully made;*

*your works are wonderful, I know that full well"* (Psalm 139:14). Remember, you're a gift to the people in your life. That gift is being the kind of person God wants you to be. You need to care for yourself and be wise with what you feed yourself. You can help the inside you by being careful with the things you listen to, what you watch on television, and the people you admire.

God loves you unconditionally, but you've got work to do, too. Renew your mind by finding out what the Bible says. When we think and look at things the way God does, according to His Word and wisdom, we will build a relationship with God that is visible to everybody around us. Trust that God *made* you very special so you are very special.

## *What We Choose*

You want to do a bungee jump. A fantasy come true! You go to the bridge, they hook you up, and faster than you can say, "Wow! This is, like, really high," they put you on the edge. What happens next? Well, that's really up to you. You could get unhooked and go home or you could go for it! Once you decide to jump there's no turning back. You put your complete trust in that rope around your feet.

Your parents and your church leaders are your spiritual bungee cord team. They prepare you for a life with God, but it's you who makes that final decision to jump into God's will. God wants you to love Him freely—He won't force you. Choosing God's will over your own is as big a mental step as that bungee leap. You have to trust that God's going to be there for you. He's got big plans for you.

We continually make choices, decisions, and commitments concerning our relationship with God. God's will and our will should be the same. Jesus taught us a lot about God's will. He even asked us to pray for God's will. *"Your kingdom come, your will be done on earth as it is in heaven"* (Matthew 6:10). Choose God's will over your own. Jesus made that choice, *"Yet not my will, but yours be done"* (Luke 22:42). Make a clear decision to be obedient to God's will, and be committed by actually doing God's will, and you'll be making the best and biggest stewardship decision of all.

# What We Do With Our Time

It took you three seconds to read this line—maybe even less. Add up all those seconds, here and there, and before you know it, *poof*, there goes a lifetime of seconds. Time is like money. You can spend it on important things or on junk. The trouble with time is you can never get it back. Once you've spent that hour between 1:00 and 2:00 P.M. on May 20, 2001, you can never recover it. So the trick of time is using it to the best of your abilities and using it the way God wants. Make every minute count. If you do that, you will have made for yourself a lifetime of rewarding experiences.

Organize your time by putting God in control of it.

(1) Do things with your time that God approves of (including not wasting it).
(2) Set aside time to really get to know God through prayer, Bible study, and church.
(3) Spend your time following God's plan for you.

# What We Own

That means everything we own, our possessions and treasures. God wants us to see that we're really managing His things. He gives us an abundance to show His love for us and to make it possible for us to show our love for Him and the people around us.

God wants us to balance how we use what He gives us between helping others, enjoying our lives, and learning to sacrifice or give things up to share His love with others. He also wants us to learn how to take care of the things He gives us so they'll last as long as possible and be there when we need them.

Don't get too focused on, "Everything's for me, me, me." Remember share, share, share. As you might have guessed, God's very big on sharing. Jesus taught us that if someone asks for our shirt we should give him our coat as well. In other words, we should be eager, ready, and willing to share our things with others. Everything we have is God's and God is always generous. When we do things His way we're generous too. With everything!

# What We Are Able to Do

Imagine you're a rock. If you were a rock, your abilities and the daily things you could do would be rather limited. You sit there. You're not exactly a fountain of activity. Thankfully, you aren't a rock. In truth, we would need a super computer to calculate all the endless possibilities of your abilities. You're very complex. God has selected outstanding talents and abilities for each of us to be good at. Sometimes it takes years of study, practice, or investigation before we perfect the abilities God has given us.

Oftentimes, the things we love to do help us discover our natural talents, whether it's sports, art, music, or other special abilities and aptitudes. As a good steward, give both your abilities and your life back to God to use. He will match your unique and complex abilities to His plan for you. And there you go—a perfect match! Tell God you want His plan and then just be the best you can be at everything you do.

Stewardship is an impressive word. To get right down to it, it's a pretty impressive way to live. Putting stewardship in action is putting God right in the action.

# #5—Stewardship Attitude

# The Attitude Leap

When you stand on that bungee bridge looking down into that deep canyon, a few thoughts are racing through your head. Mainly, "What am I doing up here?" and "Should I or shouldn't I?" You have to decide to let go of your fears and concerns. Our walk with God is like that, too! A million questions race through our heads, a million concerns, a million doubts. If we let those things cloud our thoughts it's hard for God to get in there and encourage us in His way. A good stewardship attitude is one that lets go of all those millions of doubts and trusts God completely. We take that leap of faith and obedience. We do things God's way because we trust in His love and we want Him to be in charge. God's way is an experience we will never forget. Just kick back and enjoy the great feeling of free-falling with God. God's got you safe in the palm of His hand.

# No Second Thought Attitudes

Trusting God is not always easy. Sometimes it may feel like you're standing on the edge of a cliff with no safety line. It may seem like things are not going to turn out the way you'd hoped. Those old questions start buzzing in your head again. What if this happens? What if that happens? What should I do about this money problem or what if I don't have the finances for this or that? Stop. When God's looking after you, you don't need to have second thoughts or worry. You've done God's will—so get excited about what He'll do next in your life. Choose to trust! We don't need to struggle with things because God's handling the ride. Just take one day at a time, be obedient to what you know to do, and trust that God is in control of your life and financial future no matter what. Our worry-free attitude about life is one of the biggest ways that we can show the light of Jesus in our lives. That's attitude in action!

# The Time-Attitude-Space Continuum

The right attitude can make our own personal universe orderly. Every part of our lives does what it's supposed to do. With the right attitudes, our lives and money matters are stable and right with God. The time-attitude-space continuum is about quantum control—how you control your high-energy feelings and viewpoints about different areas of your life. Let's look at this scenario. You know you should spend some important time with God, your family, and school, but you'd rather just do what you want to do. Your attitude is, "If it's my life, why can't I do what I want?" With that kind of attitude, your time-space continuum is warping quickly. You may find yourself in an alternate universe of poor time management, and lack of self-control.

You need to do a quantum leap into a new continuum by getting a right attitude. The stable time-attitude-space continuum is, "I know God loves me. He wants me to use my time in a balanced way. So that must be the best way to do it." This new stable and proven theory concludes that we understand that God does know best. And His best is our best. We want to manage our time the way He wants.

# The Money-Attitude-Space Continuum

The money-attitude-space continuum theory is based on the same principles as the time-attitude continuum theory. We need to take that same quantum leap with our attitude toward money. We have to go from a "my money universe" to a "God's money universe." How we use our money shows us our attitude toward stewardship. It's a clear, concrete, in-your-face indicator. We need to explore what God wants us to spend our money on. Our money use, just like our time use, has to be balanced. If our money starts getting sucked into selfish black holes, we're in for some real trouble. God wants us to be generous. Test the money-attitude theory by giving today. It will open up a whole new universe.

# #6—Tithing: The Giving Gift

# Tithing-O-Gram

You've given it a lot of thought. You've paced around your room for hours. You want to give God a gift. What can you give God? He seems to be the type that already has everything. Even if you could find something, how would you get it to Him? In the Old Testament, people gave this a whole lot of thought. They probably paced around their tents for hours. So you see, you're not the first one to consider this problem.

God has given us the ability, through our talents and career, to make money. Prosperity or wealth is a gift from God. How do we say thanks to God? Send Him a tithing message. When we give some of our money to the church to use, we are saying thank you to God. When we tithe, we give our church the resources to put God's will into immediate action. By tithing, we are helping to build God's kingdom.

Giving some of our money to the church is, amazingly, like a special delivery gift straight to God. It is our way of saying thanks for everything. *"Honor the Lord with your wealth, with the firstfruits of all your crops; then your barns will be filled to overflowing, and your vats will brim over with new wine"* (Proverbs 3:9–10). Wait a minute—who said anything about farming? In the Old Testament, a person's wealth was measured by the animals he raised and the crops he grew. Today we measure our wealth or income in the form of money.

# How Much?

How many cows or how much money are we talking about giving away? Tithe is an Old English word that means "tenth." God told us way back, when our money was running around on four legs, to give back 10 percent of our wealth. He didn't mean the runty animals, or the not-so-good, slightly bruised, fruit. Nope, God wants first picks. That means giving Him the best, or, in our case, 10 percent right away before we spend our money on anything else. We can give more than 10 percent. That's just a starting place. We also give God things besides our money, like our time, energy, and skills.

So, you've earned your money, and you want to give some of your wealth back to God. Great, but how do you get it to God's house? There's that delivery problem again. You don't even have the zip code? Surprise! We're talking about people. We are the church. Each one of us is part of the church. God's purpose for His people is to spread His Word and build His kingdom. We have a responsibility to support Christians doing God's will. God gives you 100 percent of your money, so giving 10 percent back to your church doesn't seem like very much. What does your church do with your money? Your money helps pay for the minister, the youth programs, the building, missionaries, and all the other great works your church is involved with.

Before you think that God has a million angels with accounting degrees checking your tithing down to the last penny, think again. The amount is not the important thing to God. Jesus once saw a very poor lady give just a small amount. He was blessed by her because He knew what a sacrifice she was making. What she gave was tiny compared to what was given by the wealthy. Yet Jesus judged her not by cash amounts, but by attitude amounts. Your stewardship attitude is what really matters to God. He wants you to tithe, not just because it is the right thing to do, but most importantly because you want to. A desire to tithe shows God we understand He owns everything and we want to thank Him for taking care of us so well. You know, a Tenth In Thanks to Him for Everything. Tithing is a celebration of God's goodness! That desire to give is the heart of the matter. Tithing really is giving from the heart.

# CHAPTER

## 2

# Money

# #7–What Is Money?

# Money Madness

There is something about money that makes people's eyes light up. Maybe it's because you can do so many things with changeable, reusable money. You can spend money, own money, lose money, win money, find money, use money, work for money, talk money, and, oddly enough, sometimes money even talks back. We like money so much we even give it pet names like bucks, dough, moola, bread, green stuff, cash, and loot. Money makes people do bizarre and silly things. Why has this invention got most of the world crazy about it?

Money today is a complex thing with an army of computers sending it around the world in a flash. Huge office towers full of workers, in every city, handle the flow of money from place to place and person to person. The government even prints new money every day. People spend years in universities just to learn how money works. But money in its early days was invented to make our lives simpler, not more complex.

# The Big Trade

Have you ever traded stuff at school like sandwiches or sports cards? Your swap is a business transaction called bartering. Thousands of years ago, every business transaction was a trade without money.

The straight product trade is easy. You have a sports card your friend wants, and he has a sports card you want, so you do the swap-o-rama. Equal trade is exchanging items of equal value.

The trade of a product for a service is a little tricky. Say your friend has the sports card of your dreams. You go for an easy equal trade. You show him your cards, but he doesn't want any of them. You can't do a trade and that's a problem. You have an idea! You offer to do his paper route for a week. He gives the idea some thought. He likes it. Bingo—you have yourself a deal. You just traded your services for a product.

That's how business was done for a long time. People exchanged services or products the old "I'll give you ten chickens for your one pig" way. Kind of like swapping sandwiches while they're still running around. This sounds like a good, workable system, but as people and towns got more complex, so did the system.

# Money Isn't Chicken

The year is 1000 B.C. somewhere in northern Europe. Meet farmer John and his wife Helga. Helga looks around the hut and decides she needs to go to the village to get a few things. John sighs. He loads up the family wagon with about three messy cages of upset chickens.

The family goes off to market. Every time Helga wants something, John has to drag some really annoyed chickens out of his wagon. Helga stands around, chatting and bargaining, convincing everyone she wants something from, that they actually need her angry chickens. Meanwhile John is covered in feathers, which is probably the reason to this day some men prefer not to shop.

The problem with trading is each party has to need the service or product the other is trading. At some point in history money was invented, maybe by our feather-covered friend John. People began to carry around little metal pieces that represented a certain value. Money allows people the freedom of buying things without having to worry about whether the seller also wants something of theirs—not to mention that a pocket full of coins is easier to carry. Well, this easy money thing made the exchange of services for products a snap. People's working relationships with each other grew and flourished. Businesses and labor had real, constant, and measurable value. You could get a set amount for your product or service. You had a cash salary and that's something to cluck about! Doing business became much more unencumbered. That freedom is something you enjoy today when you get paid in cash for your pizza delivery or other jobs. This money idea changed history. The rulers of ancient countries started organizing the value of money (probably because they were tired of chickens running around the palace) and how it would look. They produced official governmental coins. Presto chango! We have money and it sure beats live chickens.

# #8—Money: How Does It Work?

# Gold

To understand how money works, we have to understand people's love of gold. Gold and silver have been the measure of a ruler's wealth for thousands of years. The gold found in your own jewelry may have been remelted and refashioned a hundred times before. Why gold? Gold is the most easily shaped metal in the world. It looks good, it doesn't corrode like many other metals, it's rare, and you can mine it easily. The desire for gold has run through history like a fever. The Klondike gold rush sent thousands of men into the unknown frozen territories of the North. They wanted to use gold as a way to get-rich-quick. They searched for wealth and many never returned. They learned too late that the love of God, not gold, is the right direction.

# Gold Standard

Gold has always equaled power. The "gold standard" is a money system that uses a fixed weight of gold to measure the value of the paper money or the coins we print. Putting it very simply, every dollar you own represents a certain weight of gold. Remember farmer John and his chickens? Say John made a paper dollar worth ten chickens. John had better have the ten chickens somewhere to back up his dollar. If he doesn't have the chickens, that dollar isn't worth anything.

Governments have the same problem as John. They need to have enough gold to represent every dollar they make. Imagine if everybody who had a U.S. dollar bill went to the government and demanded gold for it. Each government should have all the gold that its money represents. Fort Knox is one of the United States's gold depositories which stores gold bars or gold bullion worth billions of dollars. So the value of gold equals the value of money. Does this system still work today? We'll find out later.

# The Money and I

Here's a twist! Did you know you can buy money? Talk about a brain overload! We can buy money with things. Farmers buy money with the crops they grow, or the animals they raise. Just about anything can be used to buy money. If you can sell it, you can get money for it.

You can also buy money with your talents. Musicians buy money with their performances, and doctors with their medical know-how. As long as people want to trade money for your abilities, you can buy money with those abilities.

You don't have to be stuffed full of amazing talents to buy money. Time can also buy money. Every hour you work at your job buys you money. Depending on your job, your hour can be worth a few dollars or thousands of dollars.

You have the power to increase what your hour is worth. You can work smarter. In 1903, Henry Ford caught onto the working smarter idea big-time. Henry wanted to make those new contraptions called automobiles. It was slow going. For one man to make one car took one big chunk of time. Henry wasn't satisfied. He incorporated a new system of interchangeable parts and an assembly line of workers to construct cars. Assembly-line car production meant Henry's company could produce more cars for less time and for a cheaper price. Henry had increased his company's worth by working smarter. Henry was happy, and so were his well-paid employees.

Working harder is another way to increase your money buying power. Let's flash back to history again for an example. The Pony Express was a mail service that started between Saint Joseph, Missouri, and Sacramento, California on April 3, 1860. The mail was carried by horseback. Each rider raced over seventy-five miles a day.

Let's look at this from a "work harder" point of view. It took the mail ten days to reach the end of the line. Each rider had to ride their hardest and if one rider failed, they all failed. The harder the riders worked, the more their company was worth. People would pay more money for a faster and more reliable service. The reputation of the Pony Express riders grew. Working harder made that service a legend.

How can we increase our working value in our own lives? We can either work more hours or pack more work into the hours we have. We can also train ourselves so that the value of each hour is greater. To get more you must increase your working value. That's value for your money!

Working harder and smarter will increase your money buying power, and your reputation as a good businessperson. When we use God's gifts wisely and to the best of our abilities, good things happen. *"His master replied, 'Well done, good and faithful servant! You have been faithful with a few things; I will put you in charge of many things. Come and share your master's happiness!'"* (Matthew 25:21).

# #9—Money History

# Try to Put That in a Coin Roller

When the Bible talked about a person's wealth, it referred to things we wouldn't even consider today. Take a look at Job's financial portfolio. *". . . and he owned seven thousand sheep, three thousand camels, five hundred yoke of oxen and five hundred donkeys, and had a large number of servants"* (Job 1:3). Give that to a banker today and he'll send you to the zoo.

Animals as money puts a whole new meaning on calling heads or tails. When you use animals or crops as money, their worth can vary. You can have a thin camel or a healthy camel. A young ox or a really old ox. Each animal and crop had to be evaluated by the buyer. The seller and the buyer then had to agree on the worth of that individual animal. The process for trading goods was a long and difficult venture. What would happen if you traded a good camel for an ox that died the next day? That could put a strain on some of your business relationships.

In most of our transactions today, we just have to look at a price tag, not the teeth of a camel. Money makes trading or bartering in services and products a whole lot easier. A dollar bill can't be healthy or sickly. If a dollar's a little ratty, who cares? It's worth the same amount as a freshly printed bill.

# Money: A Toss of Inventiveness

The idea of trading rare or valuable items for things was the start down the money highway. Villages would trade highly prized items such as shells, stones, metals, salt, spices, rare woods, and animal teeth, bones, skins, or feathers. If it was in high demand, it could be traded. This was great, but how did you compare all these different items? Was a dog tooth worth two shells? Who decided? This problem of value increased as great trade routes emerged, expanded, and converged across the known world. A system of easily comparable values was needed. Where there is a need, there is an invention to answer the call: Money!

When did this amazing invention called money happen? We'll never know when the first coin got tossed, but archaeology has pointed us in the direction of western Turkey around 640–600 B.C. That's around six hundred years before Jesus was born in Bethlehem. These inventive Lydians, as they were called, made bean-shaped nuggets out of a mixture of silver and gold. It didn't take long before merchants and traders spread the idea to the other kingdoms. Virtually everybody was making their own coins just one hundred years later. Hand-struck coins were *in* and happening. The Greeks took the idea of coins and made them . . . well . . . very Greek. The Romans, not to be outdone by their neighbors, not only put the portraits of their rulers on their coins but also produced coins with a standard size, weight, and value. Coins themselves soon became works of art with portraits of emperors or gods on them, or inscriptions naming the country the money was made in and sometimes the ruler. We know that by Jesus' time coins were pretty standard items. Jesus discusses a Roman denarius with the Pharisees in Matthew 22:19–22. It had Caesar's portrait and inscription on it.

The history of money shows a wide variety of coin sizes, shapes, weights, artwork, and metals. Coins got really "big" (in size, that is) after the discovery of the New World (North America). This new wealth of gold and silver encouraged the production of large silver coins. Durable, long-lasting, metal money was here to stay. When we compare coins to their more recent partner, paper money, coins are the heavyweight winners. A coin's life span can be thousands of years. Now that's money with staying power! To find out more about coins you could become a *numismatist* (coin collector). It just might be worth it . . .

## *Here Today, Coin Tomorrow*

Today, modern coin mints produce well over ten thousand coins every two minutes. Money is a high-tech international industry producing billions of dollar bills and coins. Now we have to ask ourselves if money is going the way of the faithful chicken. Computers send financial transactions around the world in the blink of an eye, neither party ever glimpsing or feeling the cool touch of a coin in their hands. Cold, hard cash is giving way to hot electronic wires.

# #10—Money Power

# Money Works

Why do we need money? Well, try walking into a department store with a crate full of chickens. Chances are you'll be escorted right out again. Money is the system we use to trade goods and services. With money we pay for our food, clothes, and all the other things we need.

Is getting lots of great stuff and having a comfortable life all there is to money? No way! Money helps us meet our daily needs, but it should also help the church get the main message out. We want our money working to deliver the gospel and to demonstrate God's love by caring for and helping others. God wants us to be cared for and He also wants us to care for others.

How can *you* help? Start in your everyday life by helping an elderly neighbor with the garden or by donating a can of soup to the local food bank. The little things you already do make a difference. Jesus has a lot to say about generosity of the heart in Matthew 25:35–36,40. When we help others it's like we're helping Him.

Your tithing does help, but don't let that stop you from doing more. Are there some areas of need that tug at you to help? Go for it! Make a regular money and/or time gift to support worthy Christian organizations in your city that run food banks, homes for single mothers, inner-city youth programs, and many more. If you want to reach out a little further, you can financially "adopt" a child from another country or support missionaries there. You can put joy and hope into the lives of people you've never met. If God can feel the pain of the needy, He can feel their joy even more. As God's money manager, you can be His ambassador of giving.

Just because money starts with the letter *m* doesn't mean it also stands for *me, mine,* and *more.* People that have a "mine" mentality put every penny they earn into buying nicer cars, bikes, and other stuff. Jesus told a story about a rich farmer who was making plans to build bigger barns for bigger crops. God had blessed this man with a successful farm and a good life. Instead of sharing His blessings with others, this guy was planning to keep it all to himself for the rest of his life. Well, God called him a fool! *"This very night your life will be demanded from you. Then who will get what you have prepared for yourself?"* (Luke 12:20). God was angry with this selfish man's attitudes and choices. Jesus warns, *"This is how it will be with anyone who stores up things for himself but is not rich toward God"* (Luke 12:21).

The "more" mood is another problem. Some people, no matter how much God blesses them, still want more. They can never be satisfied. If one car is good, then twenty would be even better. They collect more and more stuff, and pretty soon what they own is actually owning them.

When we are good stewards with the things entrusted to us, caring for them and sharing them, God is pleased and will give us more to care for and share with.

## Money Can Spread the Word

Did you know that sometimes a movie company spends as much money on advertising a movie as they did in making that movie? Millions of dollars are spent on movie advertisements. They want everybody to know about their movie.

As Christians, don't we want everybody to know about the gospel? Jesus instructed His disciples, *"Go into all the world and preach the good news to all creation"* (Mark 16:15). If most of the world has heard about the movie *Jurassic Park*, why haven't they heard about the salvation of Jesus Christ?

Well, money seems to be the problem, but it can also be a solution to getting the gospel out to the world God loves. Your good stewardship and your money can be part of that big mission. When you put your money toward God's goals you can almost hear Him applauding. Be a press agent for God by giving money to your church charities and missionaries. As they say in the communication business, help give God some "airtime."

# #11—A World of Money

# Internationally Speaking

Money has pretty much stayed the same for thousands of years. But, the names we call money, the way we count money, and the way it looks have changed. Countries from all over the world have put their own unique stamp of style on the idea of money. It comes in all shapes and sizes. Here are some countries and the money they use:

America, Australia,
    Canada, Singapore — dollar
Belgium, France,
    Switzerland — franc
Denmark, Norway — krone
Germany — mark
Great Britain — pound
Greece — drachma

India — rupee
Italy — lira
Japan — yen
Malaysia — ringgit
Mexico — nuevo peso
South Korea — won
Spain — peseta
Thailand — baht

From an international point of view, having all this variety causes some banking headaches. How do we conduct business with another country with a totally different money system? We discussed the gold standard—a dollar equals a weight of gold. Modern money is valued by a system described as "managed currency." The amount of gold a country has is considered, along with the country's purchasing power and the way that government manages its resources and credit. Basically, how well that country keeps shop determines how much its money is worth.

With different money worth different amounts floating around the world, how can we do business with each other? The system of foreign exchange helps convert one type of money into another by measuring each country's managed currency and rating it in terms of which is worth more. Every day this money rating chart changes depending on how each country is managing its affairs. Sound complicated?

If you wanted to exchange your U.S. dollar for Malaysian ringgits, the bank would tap into the foreign exchange rate for that day. The rate compares the two currencies. Suppose your dollar is worth more than a ringgit. When you go to that country, your dollar buys you more. But this won't always be the case. Currencies are changing their positions constantly.

# An Exchange of Caring

As you can imagine, this is a complex business. When a country is not managing its business well, the consequences for its people can be devastating. Mismanagement can lead to civil wars, no jobs, sickness, and poverty.

The Bible story of Joseph and his success in Egypt is about a country being prepared. Pharaoh put Joseph in charge of managing his country. Joseph listened to God and was obedient to His will. He stored the grain from seven years of good harvests and prepared the country for seven years of famine. Joseph's wise management saved the people of Egypt from starvation. Unfortunately, many countries today haven't been as wise.

When Joseph's brothers traveled from Canaan to Egypt to get food, Joseph gave them all the things that they needed. We should be like Joseph by sharing our own prosperity with others. God didn't make Joseph or Egypt rich just for their sake. When the famine came they shared their wealth with the world. Our generosity and helping others through Christian works spreads God's kingdom around the world, country by country.

# Exchange Power

This problem of stronger or weaker money can be used to help people. We live in a country with a strong economy and a strong dollar. Our strong dollar has excellent buying power.

Maybe this real-life story can explain: A businessman traveling through a foreign country saw some women picking rice in a field. The tropical trees, swaying rice plants, and women made for a beautiful photograph. The businessman asked to take their picture. The women agreed. To thank them, the man reached into his pocket and took out some change. He gave it to the women. They screamed in amazement and rushed off to tell their families. The businessman was confused until his guide explained that his loose change was two months' wages to these hardworking women.

Our dollar, which only buys a soft drink here, can buy clothes, medicine, and so much more overseas. It doesn't take much money by our standards to change the world for someone else. So, every day, take some of your loose change and put it aside for mission work around the world.

# #12—Employment

GARDENER

TEETH FLOSSING

CARPENTRY

# The Community Beat

In order for us to give and help we need to earn money. How do we do that? Employment equals earning, and earnings equals the ability to share. Ever notice that when you hurt a certain part of your body, say, your thumb, you feel it more and then seem to notice it a lot more? You're not really using your thumb more, you're just more aware of using it because of the pain. Your body is a complex system of different cells all doing different jobs. Heart cells contract to make the heart pump, the blood cells carry oxygen to the body, and the cells in your eyes react to light. Every part of your body has a job to do, and every part contributes to the amazing thing called the human organism. It is a community of parts working together.

Your town works just like a human body. Different jobs contribute to the community in different ways. The grocery provides food (like the stomach), the policeman provides order (like white blood cells), and the road workers help make transportation between businesses possible (veins). Each business is important to the health of the community. When we enter the workforce, we enter into a role that serves and contributes to the community. Employment links people and places together. It's the community beat.

# Employment

What is employment? When someone employs you, they are entering into a contract with you. You are offering them your time, talent, or abilities in exchange for something else (like money payment). People have been on both sides of that contract for thousands of years. As long as there have been employers there have been employees.

What we trade our services for, however, has changed over the last two thousand years. In the Old Testament, poor Jacob worked for Laban for fourteen years to marry Rachel (Genesis 29:6–30). Things have changed a little since then. You don't see too many people lugging home donkeys at the end of the month. Animals and crops just aren't part of our paychecks. We use that ever-useful invention called money as our main form of service payment.

The jobs we do have changed over the years as well. Our

careers are evolving and transforming at an alarming pace. Jobs that were useful a year ago are not useful today. Trying to train and keep pace with modern technology can be tough. What type of jobs are in our future? What will be a valued product or service in the future?

Whether we are shoeing horses or designing computer chips, the idea of trading a service for a product is constant. Just like the human body, a community can't function unless it has a variety of jobs that fill a variety of needs. Need is an important part of employment. If nobody in your community needs your service, nobody will trade with you. Even in your own town you can observe businesses opening and shutting down. There are many reasons for an unsuccessful business, but when you boil it down, often there is no need for that service. Your job has to fill a community function. Failure or success is often measured by your ability to help your community. When studying a business you want to work for, or a career you want to train in, this concept of service and demand should be one of the things on the top of the list for you to consider, right up there with your gifting and God's calling. But we'll talk about that later. An expert sheepshearer in New Zealand will find lots of work. An expert sheepshearer in New York City is going to have some empty pockets and a lot of free time.

OK, you found a job that everybody needs. Before you get started you better do some research. Oops—you find out there are already twenty other businesses just like yours, and they are all competing for the same customers. You can either move to a community that needs you, or try something else. Some cities even put a limit on certain businesses so there aren't too many of them. Community, service, need, and employment are all part of the business world.

# #13—Business

# Size Doesn't Matter

A business either produces a product, or provides a service. Today, money is the product we trade our products or services for. This combination of service and products has endless possibilities. The standard today is, of course, that you create a product or service and you get paid in that all-purpose product called money. What product you produce or what service you provide can be anything as long as you have a buyer for it.

When we think of business, we tend to think about *big* businesses like McDonald's, Coke, or Microsoft. These companies make more money than some countries. They employ thousands of men and women, they sell billions of their products a day, and they have outlets in every imaginable spot on Earth. They are enormous! Yes, those are businesses, but so is the lemonade stand down the block. Size is not a factor in deciding what a business is. Big or small businesses provide the earning power that help you give for God. Business basics are not complicated once you take the time to put all the parts together.

# The Business Puzzle

Business is doing something that makes you money. You are thinking, "That sounds easy. Let's go!" There are a number of different problems you have to consider before you can start your own business. Don't worry, it's just like a puzzle. Start with one piece, then add another and another. Pretty soon you have, with prayer, sweat, and the help of your superior brain, produced a unique and earth-shattering product or service. Now, what do you charge for it? Well? There are a number of questions you have to plug into that computer brain of yours:

(1) How much did it cost to make this product?
(2) How many employees do you need?
(3) How much do you need to pay them?
(4) How many of these wonder gadgets do you need to sell to cover all your expenses?
(5) How much do you need to charge per product in order to cover your expenses and make a small profit?
(6) Do you have a market for your product?

(7) Is your market a long-term investment or a quick fad?
(8) Can you deliver your product to your customers?

Business isn't as easy as it looks. All these questions and, most importantly, their answers, will determine if your business is a success. If your answers satisfy you, then maybe your business has the right stuff and you will succeed. It doesn't matter if you want to start and run your own business or work for someone else—both help the community system work. We need both!

The right to start and fail at business is one that has been passed on through the many generations of entrepreneurs. An entrepreneur is someone who is willing to risk his wealth and future on a business idea. Entrepreneurs have always relied on the free enterprise system. The *free enterprise system* is not the next series in the *Star Trek* saga. The free enterprise system is the idea that every individual has a right to pursue a means of earning money. The right, in other words, to set up shop. This system means that government or rulers can't force you to pursue a business, or become employed by a business that you have no interest in. You can pursue any business you want as long as there is a need and a demand for your product or service.

The business you do, and the way in which you do it, should all reflect God's presence in your life. As a Christian, you should add that to the top of your business importance list. Before you step into business or start your career planning, bring it to God in prayer. Remember, you are a steward in this life. God wants you to know that He has a plan for you. The best plan going!

# CHAPTER
## 3

# Attitude

# #14 — The Right Attitude

# Our Attitude

The Bible is a very cool book. It is full of stories, battles, people, miracles. . . . It has more action in it than any movie. The Bible is also full of people with very different attitudes. Pharaoh, Job, Samson, and Esther were real-life people with different views on things, and good and bad attitudes. Through their life stories, we discover God's teaching and His heart; as well as the way He deals with us, our lives, relationships, jobs, and financial matters.

# Armchair Advice

How many times have you watched a sports event where it was very clear what the player should have done? We groan, sigh, and wonder why they didn't see it too. It was obvious, right? Reading the Bible can be a lot like watching sports or a movie. It's easy for us to see everybody's attitudes. We can see that not letting the Israelites go was not a smart move on Pharaoh's part. We know his attitude was all wrong. Why didn't this guy figure it out sooner, right?

From the armchair we are wonderful athletes, dancers, actors, directors, counselors, and any number of other things. Why is that? Well, we're not involved. It's easy to look at other people and see their mistakes. Jesus had a few things to say about the armchair quarterback. *"How can you say to your brother, 'Brother, let me take the speck out of your eye,' when you yourself fail to see the plank in your own eye?"* (Luke 6:42). See the problem? What about our own attitudes . . . ?

# Attitude: How Do We Get One?

Attitudes are funny things—we can sport an attitude, *change* it, and even lose it. An attitude is like a chameleon, a small African lizard that changes color. It changes its colors in response to things that are happening around it. A chameleon responds to light, temperature, and mood. It reveals its inward reaction to us by its outward change in color. Cool.

Our attitude is the same way. We react to people and events with a whole range of emotions and attitudes during the course of our day. Like the chameleon, our body language, what we say, and what we do all show the world our inside thoughts. It's the way we change colors.

Attitudes show how we feel inside. Unlike the poor chameleon, we can consciously pick which attitude we are going to have when we meet life's challenges. Picking and choosing our responses is a complicated process. How we react to people and events is a banner declaring our internal values. We can choose to be angry with someone, or we can choose to forgive that person. "Oh yeah! He made me angry!" Sound familiar? Nobody can make you angry. It's always your choice.

We can start out with one type of attitude and consciously change it to another. This is a learning process. The Bible is our manual on which attitudes God values. We can sit in our armchairs and study the lives and events in the Bible. We can learn what attitudes please God. We make a choice to have right, godly attitudes that work. They make life more enjoyable, and they make *you* more enjoyable, too. People just want to be around someone with a positive outlook and a great attitude. Bad attitudes and a negative outlook separate us from God, family, friends, and coworkers. They can also hinder our ability to be good stewards. Pretty scary.

Because of the teaching in the Bible, we don't have to go out and make the same mistakes that, say, Pharaoh did. God's Word is like a mirror that can show us where we need to grow and how we should live our lives. Paul knew that when he wrote, *"Follow my example, as I follow the example of Christ"* (1 Corinthians 11:1).

After reading the Bible, you still need help choosing and controlling your attitudes. God sees your inner heart and knows you're trying. Pray to God about your attitudes and actions. He's there to help. *"Don't let anyone look down on you because you are young, but set an example for the believers in speech, in life, in love, in faith and in purity"* (1 Timothy 4:12).

# #15—The Three Wise Attitudes

# Light Attitudes

Are you a kaleidoscope of attitudes? If you focus in on the attitudes God desires for you, it will be easier to see the big picture. When we have godly attitudes, we are better friends, students, workers, money managers, and stewards.

# Honesty

Honesty is something you don't notice until you lose it. Ever get that awful sinking feeling when you lose something precious? When you lie, it is just like you lost your honesty—and honesty is a precious thing.

When you are truthful, it's like walking around in a clean white shirt. You have nothing to be ashamed of. You can shake the pastor's hand with pride. When you lie, it's like you just dumped grape juice on that shirt. Sure, you could try to cover up the stain by pulling your tie over it or by brushing your hair to cover it, but sooner or later things are going to shift. Bingo—there's that stain again. The harder you try to cover it up, the more you worry about it. Pretty soon covering up lie-stains becomes a full-time job.

We can lie to ourselves. We can lie to others. But remember this, every time you lie you are going against the way God created things to work. The Bible says God is Truth.

There are many reasons we shouldn't lie. When we lie, we show we don't trust God, we hurt the people that trust us, and we lose respect. When we lie, that's the first thing people notice about us. People take one look at our stained shirt and don't even want to know the person in that shirt.

Let's name that shirt your character. Now, let's give names to those large purple spots: dishonest, untrustworthy, unreliable, hurtful, self-centered, ungodly, and disrespectful. That's a heavy list of words and attitudes.

Dishonesty is a messy business. How do we get our shirts clean again? That's simple. We ask Jesus and those we hurt to forgive us. Be more careful next time. If we make honesty part of our lives, our character doesn't have to go through the mud.

What happens when we are honest? We stay right with God. People at home and in our communities see us as people that they want to spend time with. People will trust us with their time, business, and money. They will put their faith in us. We have earned ourselves a good character and a good reputation.

# *Integrity*

When we lie, we've lost that other important thing called integrity. *"The man of integrity walks securely, but he who takes crooked paths will be found out"* (Proverbs 10:9). Integrity is being true to a set of morals and values. In other words, we believe in a Christian life and we follow God's laws and instructions. When we have integrity, we can be close to God. Lack of integrity divides us from God. It makes us feel like there's a big canyon between us and our Maker. Integrity is part of the godly bridge to having a right attitude, keeping safe, maintaining a good reputation, and improving our personal and business relationships. If we can be trusted, people will work with us and will even promote us. Integrity is the highway to success.

# *Ethics*

Have you ever heard someone say, "He has absolutely no ethics!" Is ethics something you have or you don't have? Can you remove a person's ethics like you can their tonsils? Ethics means believing in certain principles and laws and living your life according to them. When we are ethical, it means we are doing things in such a way that it reveals what we believe to others. Somebody who is ethical talks the talk and walks the walk. You can talk about what you believe—that's easy. But what counts is doing what you believe—actually doing what God wants you to do and showing people that you are following God's teachings in your everyday activities. You can think of your ethics as a marquee sign advertising My Walk with God; produced, directed, and written by God. Starring me. Costarring honesty, integrity, trust, and generosity. The only person who can compromise your ethics is you. Remember, being ethical is acting ethically.

# #16—Contentment

# The Hunt

Contentment is an attitude with mystery attached. Do you have contentment? People all over the world are looking for it. Many of them just can't seem to find it (and you didn't even know it was lost). The world views contentment like a big treasure in some secret place. Contentment isn't lost, and it certainly isn't a secret. It is just being happy with your life. That sounds easy, so why doesn't everybody have it? Everyone has to find contentment for themselves, and everybody could find it if only they looked in the right spot.

# The Spot

The spot that they should be looking in is the Bible. Like all things in our lives, the Bible is a map to the things we need. It gives three secrets to being content.

(1) *Do Things God's Way.* Have you ever been absolutely convinced you are going the right way? You head off in the direction you picked with confidence and energy. Pretty soon you realize that things don't look very familiar. In fact, you have no idea where you are. You get worried, and nervous, and you feel oddly alone. You trudge around until you're all worn out. If you had stopped and looked at God's map first, you wouldn't have gotten lost. When we follow God and do it His way, things become very clear. We know where we've been, we know what we're doing, and we know our destination. *"Your word is a lamp to my feet and a light for my path"* (Psalm 119:105). God wants to keep us on a safe and joyful path. We can help by doing things His way. Remember He created everything and He knows how it works.

(2) *Be Patient.* We live in a fast-paced society that wants everything right away. We're getting to the point where hyperfast computers are too slow, and microwave ovens don't cook quickly enough. Those are just the little things in our lives, but they spill over to big things. Why wait to save for that car or education? We can have it now on credit. We want to make lots of money using get-rich-quick ideas. Why wait until we study or train for a job?

When we don't get things fast enough, we become impatient with God. Impatience leads to unhappiness, and unhappiness leads to disobedience. *"But the people grew impatient on the way; they spoke against God and against Moses, and said 'Why have you brought us up out of Egypt to die in the desert? There is no bread! There is no water! And we detest this miserable food'"* (Numbers 21:4–5). Just like the Israelites, we wonder what's taking God so long! Faster and faster we go until we're going so fast it's scary to stop. If you've ever skied or biked out of control, you know how helpless you feel. Stop now before you crash. Give God the controls back by trusting Him to give you the things you need when He knows you should have them. Be content with God's timing. It is always perfect when we are patient.

(3) *Be Thankful!* One of the biggest barriers to finding contentment today is the desire for stuff. It doesn't seem to matter how much stuff we have. Much is never enough and more is motivating. We forget about all the things that God has already given us. When we always desire more things it makes us feel unhappy, jealous, and impatient.

We're like a kid just opening more and more presents only to throw them aside so we can open the next. *"Keep your lives free from the love of money and be content with what you have, because God has said, 'Never will I leave you; never will I forsake you'"* (Hebrews 13:5). Thank Him with all of your heart and be happy with His blessings. When we have an attitude of thankfulness we are content with the way our life is going and trust God with all our strength. It brings us closer to God.

# *Found It*

Are you wondering why all those people are having problems finding contentment in their lives? All you need is to do things God's way, trust Him, and be thankful for His gifts. Finding contentment brings great rewards. God's peace, happiness, and contentment make it easier to be good money stewards by giving, tithing, and saving. Contentment is a win-win-win attitude.

# #17—Prioritize

# *Priorities*

A priority is something that should have your attention before other things. There are as many ways to handle your priority list as there are priorities. Organizing the different parts of your life can be a handful. You have obligations at home, school, church, with friends, and at work. Who should get your attention first? How do you decide what things you should do, and how much of your time you should spend doing them? People's organizational skills can be pretty funny when it comes to daily planning. Take a look at these priority styles.

(1) *The Cluttered Room Technique.* Many of us love to have all our priorities in a big jumble. The trick is to make our lives so confusing that we don't have to worry about what should be done first because we can't find it anyway.

(2) *The Fish Bowl Method.* We put all our priorities in a bowl and just randomly pull stuff out. Every day is a surprise—we're not saying a good surprise.

Neither of these ideas works. They're confusing, unpredictable, and neglectful. We have priorities for a reason. They help us organize our lives and understand what is important. Let's take a look at money priorities. We have a hundred things in our lives—more and more as we get older— that demand money, including our tithe, bills, food, education, and clothes. Sometimes we feel there just isn't enough money for everything. We might forget what God's purpose for money is. We might even do something that we know isn't God's way because it makes more money for us. Stop! People get caught in a lifelong trap when they put aside their Christian values for the love of money. A good priority list helps keep us focused on godly money use and attitudes. When we use money the way God wants, we won't want for anything.

God's Word helps us fix our list of priorities. *"You shall have no other gods before me"* (Exodus 20:3). The Bible makes it very clear where God should be on our list—the top! Your list for time and money should be God, family, friends, school or work, recreation . . . This verse is your priority ruler.

# *What to Do?*

Priorities help us make decisions on whether we can or should do certain things. Before we do anything, buy something, or go anywhere, we should hold it up to our priority list. The priority ruler helps us stay focused on what's important but does what you want to do interfere too much with more important things? Deciding to go surfing all week may be fun, but does that leave you time to be with God, get your school project done, or be with your family? Maybe just one day of surfing would be better.

Priorities help us decide what's important and how much time we should spend on it. Take work, for instance. Work is important, but let's not let it exclude other parts of our lives. Working seven days a week may make you lots of money, but let's hold it up to the ruler. What does it support? Does it support your desire for money? Yes. Does it make your family happy? No, they never get to see you. Does it make God happy? No, He doesn't get to spend time with you either. Does it support the values that you want to live by? No. There's no room in your life for anything but money. Priority alert! Better reorganize.

Does your priority list follow God's plan for your life? God has designed our lives to have balance in all things. Our devotional time, our family, work, rest, relationships, personal time, and recreational time should, if we're following God's will, be balanced. *"There is a time for everything, and a season for every activity under heaven"* (Ecclesiastes 3:1).

Do you feel like you have too many priorities? Are you juggling things as fast as you can? God doesn't want us to be a juggling act. So stop, get your balance, and hand off those priorities by praying to God. Give yourself a break by leaving the solution to God. *"Cast all your anxiety on him because he cares for you"* (1 Peter 5:7). Have faith that God will return your priorities to you in ways that you can handle. When you make room for God, He'll make room for everything else.

# #18—The Get-Rich-Quick Attitude

# Jack's Lead

Once upon a time there was this kingdom. Everybody worked hard and the people were happy. That is, until Jack showed up. Jack lived in this OK house, and drove an OK car. The story goes down something like this. Jack liked new things a lot. The problem is, Jack didn't want to work and wait for those new things. He wanted everything now! Jack's philosophy was "Forget the past, why worry about the future, go for the now!" And he did!

He went around buying all kinds of stuff on credit. He had everything! This was living! Well, it wasn't long before this "get stuff now" attitude spread through the kingdom. Jack's neighbors and even the king got into it. It was totally crazy.

# God's Intermission

What's wrong with this story? It seems Jack and the gang have forgotten a few very basic things. Jack's philosophy goes against everything God teaches about stewardship attitude.

(1) *Working Hard Attitude.* We have to work and save for the things we need. *"He who works his land will have abundant food, but he who chases fantasies lacks judgment"* (Proverbs 12:11).

(2) *Contentment Attitude.* We should be thankful for the things we have. *"Keep your lives free from the love of money and be content with what you have"* (Hebrews 13:5).

(3) *God's Stuff Attitude.* We should be using our money wisely and with an ear to God's heart. *"And do not forget to do good and to share with others, for with such sacrifices God is pleased"* (Hebrews 13:16).

(4) *Planning Attitude.* God wants us to be planners. What you do today is your foundation for tomorrow. *"Commit to the Lord whatever you do, and your plans will succeed"* (Proverbs 16:3).

# Jack Feels the Heat

Well, Jack is over his head and we aren't talking about his pool. He has more credit cards and bank loans than any guy around and he can't make the payments. His carefree lifestyle isn't so carefree. Everyone is threatening to sue and he's a nervous wreck! Jack isn't a bad guy—he just got deceived. Jack listened to everybody except God.

Jack decides that getting-rich-quick is the only way to pay his debts. He tries magic beans, rubbing old lamps, and treasure maps. But, alas, none of these ideas pan out. Jack and the whole kingdom are in big financial and spiritual trouble.

## Kingdom of Us

Would it surprise you that Jack's kingdom is really our own society? Did you know that less than one hundred years ago buying things on credit was scarcely heard of and most everyone knew that the way to get ahead was to work hard and handle one's money wisely? How did we zip so fast from an attitude of earning, saving, and waiting for things to this trendy attitude of something for nothing and *now*? Simple, by following bad examples like Jack.

Many young people have a false sense of security because of the idea of fast money and get-rich-quick ideas. Take Jack, Jr. He's learned his money matters from his dad, and now he's looking for his own get-rich-quick ideas.

He could become a rock star, movie star, model, or professional athlete. They make huge amounts of money at younger and younger ages. The plan? Jack could learn music, hang out to be discovered, build up his muscles. All in a week. Sorry, but it isn't that easy. Let's see how the averages stack up.

- Of all high school senior basketball players, only 2.7 percent go on to play college basketball.
- Less than three in one hundred college seniors play one year of professional ball.
- Most pro-ball players have a career of three to four years.

Jack's other ideas stack up about the same, but Jack, Jr. still needs fast bucks. Bingo! Or should we say lottery? But lottery winner history shows that most winners end up back in financial trouble because they don't know how to manage money. The key isn't more money; the key is learning to follow God's principles for money handling.

## No Quick Answers

What is the solution to get-rich-quick schemes? Get-rich-slow. God's financial way is to build your lives, finances, education, and careers wisely on His teachings. Your philosophy should be to go long, go steady, and go tried-and-true.

# #19—Generosity

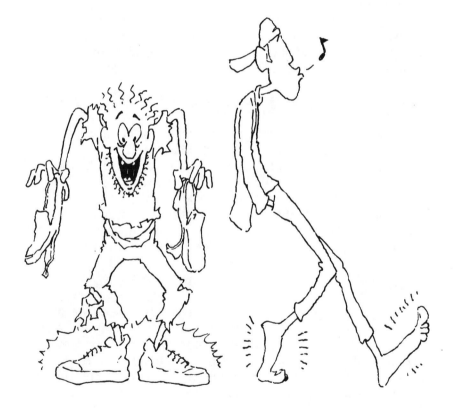

# Cityscape

Generosity is the attitude that gives us the most! Generosity is caring about other people's needs. It's taking the "me" out of our daily thoughts and replacing it with "others." It's a whole new way of looking at things. It's like a new language and a new life with a new set of rules. It's a whole new place. Let's call that place Generosity City.

People in the city don't spend their days wondering what they are going to do for themselves. Instead they wonder about what they are going to do for others. They don't plan what stuff they're going to buy. Instead they plan what they could give to others. They take time, money, love, and caring—and give it away. Sound like an unbelievable place?

You're already part of that city. It is the kingdom of God. We are instructed to be part of that kingdom even though we are still living here. God's way of thinking is very different from the world's. God's idea of being rich has money as one very small part.

# What Is Our Treasure?

*"For where your treasure is, there your heart will be also"* (Luke 12:34). The message is loud and clear! What we value reflects our hearts. Imagine if we had to sit forever in a room with the things we valued. Many of us would be sitting alone with bags of money and lots of pictures of ourselves. Think about it!

What's the alternative? How about sitting in a room full of family, friends, and strangers to whom we gave time, love, support, and caring? That's a treasure room God would be proud of.

# Giving

We know that God wants us to give, but how do we start? We already discussed tithing, and in principle, it sounds great. We're behind tithing and charity donations 100 percent—until we count out 10 percent of our income. Suddenly, bills, expenses, purchases, college savings, and buying all the things we ever wanted pop into our heads. Letting go of that hard-earned money is a little more difficult than one might think. Before you take your money back, think about who gave you that money. Aren't you glad God didn't find it that difficult when He gave it to you?

Jesus gave His entire life. That's sacrificial giving—and we need to learn from it. The more we give, the more it changes our lives. It makes us richer in spirit. A truly giving heart is willing to give up its comfort for another. What does sacrificial giving look like? It's when you give someone else your coat so they don't have to be cold (but you are). It's when you share your lunch because they forgot theirs. It's when you don't go to that sports game because Mrs. Martin needs your help getting her cat to the veterinarian. God wants us to give generously, but most importantly, from the heart. *"Remember this: Whoever sows sparingly will also reap sparingly, and whoever sows generously will also reap generously. Each man should give what he has decided in his heart to give, not reluctantly or under compulsion, for God loves a cheerful giver"* (2 Corinthians 9:6–7).

## Worry-Free Giving

Worried that you just don't have enough money and time to share? Jesus said, *"But seek first his kingdom and his righteousness, and all these things will be given to you as well"* (Matthew 6:33). Sure, helping others does change your use of money, time, and, most importantly, your outlook. But, unbelievably, it does not change your financial position. When you give generously and sacrificially, you show God that you trust His care of you and your money matters. Trusting God makes things work out better. He will respond to your trust, commitment, and sacrifice by providing more where you need more. Trust God to multiply all your good works. When you live in God's Generosity City, you are rich where it counts and God will take care of your needs. *"Through the blessing of the upright a city is exalted"* (Proverbs 11:11). You're changing lives, and God is applauding your faithfulness.

# #20—Relationships First

# Price Tag on Relationships

You want to take a hike in a beautiful valley. Everything is perfect—the sounds, the sun, the breeze through the trees. Suddenly a huge angel appears. He has a fast cash register and a list of items that you owe money for. What? He wants you to pay him for the use of the trail, trees, stream, and a viewing cost for all the animals? Wait a minute! That's not the way it works! God doesn't charge us! Is this angel confused or what? God *gave* us these gifts to enjoy. That's what God is like. You and His relationship with you are far more important to Him than things.

# What's First?

What about you? Are your relationships with the people in your life first before anything else? Do you put your love for your family before work, school, money, and time? The Bible teaches us that love is the greatest of all gifts. Nothing can separate us from God's love. Can we say the same thing about our love for others?

# The Dividing Line

Unfortunately, we do let things get in the way of our relationships with friends, family, and coworkers We can let pride, fame, self-interest, friends, and things get in the way of relationships that are important to us. One of the biggest relationship busters can be money. Money misunderstandings have a way of becoming mountains of misunderstanding. Our courts are full of ex-spouses, ex-family members, ex-friends, ex-business partners, ex-employees, ex-employers—all fighting over money issues. Everybody is so wrapped up in money that they get cut off from the really important things. Money madness can actually get us mad with each other.

Before you let money think for you, think again. Are money issues separating you from others? Is how you spend money worth a bad relationship with your folks? Should you let a loan to a friend that's not being repaid break up your friendship? The people in your life are more important than a zillion dollars. Money can be very lonely. It can isolate you from God and loved ones. There is a better way!

# Love Rules

What's going to rule our relationships with God and the people in our lives? Money or love? That is an important question! When you ask an important question, God always has the answer. When asked which of all the commandments was the most important, Jesus replied, *"The most important one . . . is this: . . . 'Love the Lord your God with all your heart and with all your soul and with all your mind and with all your strength.' The second is this: 'Love your neighbor as yourself.' There is no commandment greater than these"* (Mark 12:29–31). If you didn't notice, money wasn't mentioned at all.

# Love Center Stage

Love should be center stage in your life. Money should just be sound equipment—a tool to get things done. If the love of money is hogging the stage, tell it to exit stage right, pronto. Are you alone on that stage? No—it's hard to have a really great jam session alone! The people you love should be singing with you. With a crowded stage you should rock the house. God should be the one directing the band. Who's listening? The world, that's all. Talk about a global tour!

Money is not a bad thing. It just has its proper place and time in both your life and thoughts. Just remember, money should work for you—not the other way around. If making money is the only motivational force in your life you won't go far. Money, after all, can't buy happiness. But a strong relationship with God and your family will.

# Jesus' Advice

Good relationships with the people in our lives are worth more than gold. God deals with us with love, generosity, mercy, and forgiveness. Jesus wants us to deal with our relationships the same way. The mountain of money misunderstandings shouldn't be the place where you build your home. If it is, it sure will be lonely at the top. Build your house on God's principles and you'll always have a house full of friends and family.

# CHAPTER 4

# Planning

# #21—What Is a Plan?

# Why Plan?

Adults often ask younger people if they have a plan or if they have made plans. Many of us just nod because we don't have the foggiest idea what they are talking about. We smile, hoping that all they want to know is what we want for lunch. If your future seems a little murky, now's the time to take action. Make a plan! If you understand what a plan is, maybe you can understand how it can help you, and why you need one.

(1) A plan can mean the foundation or ground level of something, just like a building plan or blueprint is the start of a huge building. A building plan clearly shows us all the parts of the building—where the doors are, where the wiring is, and how they relate to each other. A plan is a map of your priorities. Your plan should outline different parts of your life and how they fit together, for example, your devotional time, work, and family. Your plan can be the starting point for great things in a long life.

(2) A plan also views things from the top or from above. Our plan should be based on God's plan for us. Any blueprint we design for our lives has to be based on God's instructions and His will for us.

(3) A plan can also be defined as a method for achieving an end. In other words, a plan isn't wandering around with absolutely no idea where you're going. That's not a plan, that's a maze. Mazes are in another chapter. Before you start your plan you must have a clear idea where you want to be when it's finished. An architect has a drawing or model of the building that shows what the building is going to look like and what it's going to be used for. A plan has a definite start, end, and goal. So should your life plan!

(4) A good plan is a detailed program of action—like building a house. First you dig a hole, then pour the foundation, then build the frame. There are steps to building a house and steps to building your life.

So, what is a plan? A plan helps you prepare for life. It gets you where God wants you to be and keeps you on track while you're going there. It's using God's teaching as a blueprint. A plan is putting your values and beliefs into action by setting out to accomplish God's will and plan for your life.

# *Forgot the Plan*

What happens if we fail to plan? Let's look at the tough game of football. The team huddles. The game plan is called. For each play there is a set of moves and strategies that each player has to do. If everybody does what they're supposed to do, the players should make their touchdown and accomplish their goal of winning the game. What if one player forgets his role? Crash, crunch, groan. It isn't a pretty picture. Players like that get carried off the field on stretchers and are traded next year. Living and working without some kind of understanding of what our goals are and how to achieve them is like going out onto that football field without having gone to practice, talked to the coach, learned the game, or bought the proper equipment. You are going to get hurt or worse, feel like a failure. Without a plan, we miss those easy moves, and we get blocked. Without a plan we get sidetracked from our goals. When you have no plan in your life, it makes for one long and confusing game that you can't win. If you fail to plan you are planning to fail.

God did not create you to be a failure. Remember, God designed you to to be successful! He will combine your abilities with His plan to create a lifetime of successes. That's not to say your life won't have challenges or difficulties. What it does mean is that God will prepare you for those times and will be with you each step of the way. To get in God's game you have to learn about God and His rules. Knowledge about God helps you understand His plan for you and will keep you on His track. Planning with God is the way to score those little and big successes.

# #22—Financing the Plan

# Plans

When you build a house, you have an overall plan called the blueprint. It shows you exactly what your house will look like, what supplies you need, what order to build things in, and how it all fits together. OK, that's your big overall life plan. Your house also has different sections in it. Carpenters build the frame, plumbers put in the plumbing, and electricians put in the wiring. But you can't build that house until you know how much it is going to cost and how you are going to earn the money you need to complete the job.

In your life there are areas that have their own special plans, too. You plan for parties, college, marriage, having kids, and retirement. Planning for a party, for example, is fun, because you get to meet someone nice, enjoy your friends, and it makes you feel great. What about financial planning? Many adults would say that it isn't fun, it doesn't make you feel nice, you don't enjoy it, you don't feel smart enough to do it, and it always makes you feel grumpy. People often avoid financial planning. Maybe they avoid it because they don't have the knowledge to follow a plan. You need a financial plan because most of your other goals in life require money planning. A financial budget makes all your plans, big and small, manageable. Let's see how following God's financial plan helps.

# Young Financial Architect

You think you're too young to do some financial planning? Are you kidding? Now's the perfect time to start. The average American teenager spends nearly $3,000 a year. No, seriously! Add up all the money from parents, jobs, or presents, and you have a pretty impressive figure. What's your plan for all that loot? The people who sell music, movies, makeup, and candy all have plans for your money. They want you to spend it. Keeping track of money is all a matter of who controls it—them or you. Controlling your money is called budgeting. Make sure your budget plan is a God-based plan.

# Budgeting Basics

You don't have to have a lot of money to budget! The ideas that help you control your money work if you have billions or just a few bucks. Remember, more money is not the answer, more money *control* is.

What is a budget? It's a plan for what you are going to do with your money. A money plan should support your other life plans. Without a good financial plan you may be stuck in a money rut, spinning your wheels. Let's look at some of the parts of a budget and get you moving down the money matters highway.

# Income/Outgo

Income and outgo should not mean the same as easy come/easy go. Many people get the income/outgo blues by spending their money as fast as they can. That's not budgeting money—that's blowing money. What is income? Basically income is money that is given to you or that you earn. Outgo is money that is exiting your life and traveling someplace else. What should happen between income and outgo is planning and budgeting.

# Delayed Spending

So, money comes in and money goes out of your life. The time that it rests in your sock drawer or in your bank account is called delayed spending. We need to plan so that some outgo gets delayed. That's called savings. The length of time your money sits waiting often depends on whether you have a plan or not. For people who don't, their money doesn't even touch ground between incoming and outgoing. In fact, it is faster than laser technology. Maybe that's why we use faster and faster computers to monitor our money.

If we have a life plan, then we have a purpose for our money. A budget keeps us on track with that plan and purpose. Why can't we just go to the movies every night and have fun? Hey, everyone else spends their money quickly and has fun. Yes, but you have a lifetime plan—a plan that will help every part of your life be enjoyable and keep you laughing all the way to the bank.

# #23—Savings

# Is There a Purpose to Saving?

Save your money? You didn't even know it was in danger. Yes, it is. There is a known gravitational pull that sucks money matter from your pocket into an unknown area in space called impulse buying. Scary, huh?

Part of keeping a good budget is keeping an account called "savings." If you start now, saving will become a lifelong habit. Start putting a percentage of every dollar you earn in your bank. They don't have to be huge deposits. A few dollars here, a few dollars there will do. It may not seem like much at first, but it does add up.

# The Savings Team

In the big game of finance, you are the captain of a savings team. Your team has one goal and that is to make and save you money. Ready to meet your players?

(1) *Short-Term Savings.* You got a part-time job on the weekends. Great, now you have some steady money to budget. One of the things on your wish list is a mountain bike. It's an expensive item, but one that you can save for in six months or a year. This is called a short-term savings plan. After you've made that big bike purchase, you don't need to set that money aside anymore. You can redirect that percentage of your earnings into other areas. You decided on a short-term goal, worked for that goal and achieved that goal. That is what a short-term savings plan is for.

(2) *Long-Term Savings.* Your parents may have started a long-term savings plan for your college education. Now that you are older, both you and your parents might deposit money into it. It's a long-term commitment. When you have big goals, like college, a house, or money to start a business, you need to be committed to a long-term savings plan—one that will go the distance with you.

(3) *General Savings.* We've discussed savings plans with very specific goals in mind, but what do we do about our everyday stuff? It's always a good idea to set aside some of your monthly income for the little, and sometimes not so little, surprises in life. Say you've bought a car and you've planned

and budgeted for the insurance and gas. Everything is going great until something large and kind of noisy falls out of your engine. Ouch–your repair bill is large. Are you in a panic? No, because you have your general savings plan to come to the rescue. Without careful budgeting, your car would have been up on blocks. But you have been carefully putting extra money away in your general savings. Pat yourself on the back. Stuff happens. If we have money saved for those unexpected things, we don't have to get all frantic. Remember, general savings is the flexible hero of the unpredictable.

## *Interested in Interest?*

Are you using your savings account as a spending account? Stop now while you still can. Try using your savings account as a savings account! What a great idea!

Why put your money in a bank? There are a ton of places around the house to hide your money. Roll it in tin foil and put it in the freezer. Cold cash! How about the ever popular titanium safe behind the picture? No, too obvious. The best and safest place for your money is the bank—and they *pay* you for doing it.

When you put your money in a savings account, you are allowing the bank to use your money. They pay you a fee for using your money. That fee is called interest. The amount they pay is a percentage of how much money you leave with them. The more money you save and deposit into your savings account, the more *interest* you get paid. Your money is making more money for you!

If interest is a good thing, why do you hear adults grumble and sigh about high interest rates? Interest is like the two sides of a coin. When you save your money, that's one side. The other side is when you borrow money from the bank. They give you money to use, but they charge you a fee to use it. Every month you pay the bank a little of what you borrowed plus the monthly interest fee. The borrowing fee, like your savings interest, is based on a percentage of the amount of money you borrowed. So, when we save, interest works for us, and when we borrow, we work for interest. Very interesting.

# #24—The Plan

# God's Idea

We just have to look at the lives of the people in the Bible to know that God has plans for us. Moses' life journey from floating down the Nile in a basket to eventually leading his people to freedom was not a wild fluke. When God has a plan, He carefully selects individuals to carry out His will, people who listen to Him through thick or thin and have faith in His plan for them.

What about us? Does God have a plan for our lives? No doubt. God created you and knows everything about you and everything that will happen to you. The Psalmist said, *"Your eyes saw my unformed body. All the days ordained for me were written in your book before one of them came to be"* (Psalm 139:16). Does that sound like a God concerned only about the big picture, or a God concerned with each of us as individuals? King David knew "full well" the awesome power of God in creating both David the man and David the king. *"For you created my inmost being; you knit me together in my mother's womb. I praise you because I am fearfully and wonderfully made; your works are wonderful, I know that full well"* (Psalm 139:13–14).

God views us as both the person we are and the person we'll become according to the plan He has for our lives. He's designed us all uniquely and exceptionally—down to the last detail.

God's plan for us perfectly matches who we are, our desires, skills, talents, and personalities. Giving God our lives and following His plan is the smartest thing we can do for a great life. What did the great heroes of the Bible have in common? They were listening to God even before the great events in their lives started to happen. How do we discover God's plan? Just ask. He's not trying to keep it a secret—He gives it to us day by day as we trust Him. Let God bring peace, ideas, and wisdom to your daily thoughts and plans through prayer. Read the Bible. Let the lives and actions of great people of faith motivate you.

When Noah was laughed at, or when Joseph spent time in prison, they probably had some doubts about God having a personal plan for their lives. Despite the hard times, their love for God remained and carried them through. Even though it may not seem like what you're doing now is part of any great plan, keep talking to God. Trust Him, and be patient—He's working things out.

# The Steps in God's Plan

How do you know you're doing the right things to follow God's plan? There are steps, like in any plan, that help you along the way.

(1) *Pray*. Take all your big interests and life decisions to God in prayer. Start now! Don't wait until they're on top of you.

(2) *Seek Wisdom*. Find and listen to wise counsel. Get information and advice about your ideas. What are the educational, financial, and experiential requirements to get your idea rolling?

(3) *Trust*. God doesn't play hide-and-seek with your life. Trust Him to give you clear directions and to keep you on the right track. Go in the direction you feel God is leading you. God may change things or change your goals (be comfortable with that). Relax, it's often hard to see the big picture. God may lead you in one direction to prepare you for something completely different. That's cool. God will show you when you need to adjust things.

(4) *Follow God's Will*. Be resolved to follow God's plan. Be ready to alter your plans or ideas. God may want you to change a number of areas. If you're concerned, take it to God until you solve the problem or have peace about it.

(5) *Take Steps*. God will provide you with solid steps along your life plan. He knows you can't scuba dive until you learn how to swim. God's plan for you has different resting points along the way. Be patient and obedient, and learn from each step. When the time is right, God's plan for you will knock your socks off!

# Little Right Decisions

Just as small, consistent deposits of money add up to huge savings, consistent right decisions add up to a lifetime of right choices. Make all your small decisions according to God's principles, and that will make the big decisions easier. All those right choices will lead you right where God wants you to be.

Maybe you're not sure if you're working in the right job. Let's say a customer overpays you by $10.00. Instead of keeping it, you run after her and give it back. The customer phones your boss with a good report about you. Your boss promotes you to a really interesting position in the company. Great! You see, God's plan was brought about by doing small things His way. It all adds up.

# #25—Long-Term Planning

# Life Planning

You're on vacation and it is *so great!* There are a hundred things you want to do and see. You get the map out and mark which places you want to go. You plan your day. That's short-term planning. We do short-term planning every day. It keeps us organized. Long-term planning is a little harder. Just like a long-term savings plan, this life planning is looking years into the future. Planning is different than just getting a map.

When it comes to your life, no one can just give you a map. With God's help, you have to make your own map. How do you know what type of map to make? Ask God. He has all the pertinent information. Mapping takes patience, time, and knowledge about you and what God wants for you.

When we leave for an event that we've never been to before, we should phone the host or hostess for directions. We listen and draw a map for ourselves. We should phone God when we make our life map, too. He will give us the most direct path to His house. He will also warn us about any confusing intersections. *"Direct me in the path of your commands, for there I find delight"* (Psalm 119:35). When we do get confused, we just have to recheck what we wrote on our map.

You've finished your mapping, you've listened to God, you know what direction you're going, and you know your destination. Now what? Work hard to do the things you know need to be done.

You wouldn't go on a long car trip without packing supplies. You might need food, drinks, warm clothing, first-aid kits, and mechanical tools. A big part of following your life plan is saving for those long-term goals. Our different savings plans are like those supplies. They keep us prepared and comfortable during our journey. You know you're going to need some kind of college fund later in life. Save for college now so you'll have it later when you need it. Goals aren't quite so overwhelming when you tackle them a little bit at a time.

# A Path Well Traveled

Most of the paths we travel are well-used. Take that opportunity to get wise counsel. Sit down with the adults in your life and ask them to help you with your goals. Discuss your priorities, abilities, talents, and attitudes. Find out if your goals are reasonable and attainable. See what types of things you can do along the way to help you. See if there are entry-level part-time jobs in the fields you want to follow. Are there summer jobs? Do they take volunteers? Are there any extra courses or night classes that might help in reaching your goals?

Most importantly, plan your financial goals. Without a strong financial base, many of your other goals will be impossible to reach. Plan how much you can put in your savings account each week or month to help you financially. There may be lots of little costs now, like extra courses or workshops. Later, when you go full-time to college or university, you'll have big costs. Plan financially now, not later.

Talking with adults who have gone down these paths before is smart mapping. Talk to professionals in the career areas you want to follow. After all, they've been down the same road. They can be both informative and encouraging. They can be the directional signposts along your life map.

Being prepared in life is all a matter of phoning God first, getting directions, mapping goals, and preparing for them. Stay close to God and don't leave your plan if it gets tough. Your resolve to stay on God's path will be tested. Staying close to God helps you during those times and when more tempting ideas come along. God and you have a long path to follow together, so stick close. Now if someone asks you if you have plans, say, "Yes, and not only that, I've mapped it out!" Now that's impressive. Go have lunch.

# #26—Investing

# Up and Down

People talk about good investments and bad investments. What exactly are investments? People invest money to make money. Your savings account is an *appreciating investment*, because the value is going up. You're making money.

Instead of putting your money in your savings account, you decide to invest money in an unknown artist. You buy his painting. You hope that later he will become famous and the value of his painting will go up. Well, it turns out your eye for art isn't what it should be. Your painting is going down in value. As an investor, you're not doing very well. When you don't get your money back from an investment, that's called a *depreciating investment*. The idea of investment is never to put your money into things that are going to go down in value.

Investments are good things when handled wisely. Often the safest investments are with banks and governments because they guarantee your investment. They won't lose your money, but they also pay lower interest. Here's a pretty reliable rule: the greater the potential for making money, the greater the risk of losing money. Some people put together an investment plan that involves putting a small portion of their investment money into medium-risk investments for a higher return. But they do their homework first and check out the track record of the investment and the reputation of the people behind it.

# Government Savings Bonds

A savings bond is like a loan to the government, just like when you loan your money to your bank. You lend your money to the government, and they pay it back, with interest, a few years later. Unlike your savings account, your money is locked up for a while (usually a minimum of five years).

# Mutual Funds

When you invest in a mutual fund, you are, again, letting your money work for you. This time a management-investment company takes your money and adds it to other people's money. These companies have an army of financial brains that plan to invest your money for you. When you put your money in the hands of a mutual fund, you are getting professional investment help. You will often gain a higher level of interest or return with a mutual fund compared to savings accounts and government savings bonds.

## The Stock Market

Welcome to the wonderful world of the stock market! "Playing" the stock market is a term that describes it well. As businesses become successful and more complex, they often need more money to put back into the company. They use that money as a foundation to make their company grow by buying more equipment, building new factories, or discovering more resources. If a company is managed properly, they will be able to pay back their investors with a profit. Where do some of these companies get their money and investors? You! They invite individuals or other companies to invest their money with them.

This all sounds great. A good way of making money without doing a thing. You just let the companies worry about making a profit. Sometimes the companies don't do as well as they hoped, and even though you invested in good faith, they can't even pay you back what you invested. That's the stock market "Ouch" factor.

There are stock exchange centers around the world. These centers are where buyers and sellers get together and trade shares (small investment amounts of different companies). The more successful a company, the more their shares are worth. The trick is to buy shares when a company is young, the demand for their stock or share is low, and each share doesn't cost very much. You buy and wait. When the company is doing really well (their investment share is worth more), you can sell and make a profit.

If you decide to invest in the stock market, it's a good idea to do a lot of homework first. Then only use a very small part of your savings because of the risk factor. Never invest money you don't have or can't afford to lose! If you don't want to do the research time, it is probably best if you invest in a mutual fund with a good track record and let the professionals decide which stocks are good ones.

## Why Should We Invest?

If your answer to why we invest is to make more money, that is only a partial reason. We should invest wisely as part of our savings plan to finance our life's plan.

# #27—Big Budget

# Time to Budget

Some people view budgeting as a huge wall between us and spending our money on the cool things we want. But they don't get it. Budgeting isn't a wall, it's a ladder! Budgeting is what helps you build a plan for your life. As your education, career, or business plans grow bigger, your budget ladder helps you to reach those goals and move higher up your life plan. The bigger your plans get, the more exciting it becomes. Your budgeting ladder provides you with the finances that get you to the top of God's plan for you and your career. Budgeting builds a strong financial plan for now and the future.

How do you budget? The total amount of money you earn every week, month, or year can be divided into sections. Each section gets a certain percentage of your income. Those percentages won't be equal. Your time isn't divided equally among your activities, right? You spend more time at school than you do playing tennis. You allow for priorities. There should be priorities in your money life as well.

Let's divide your income into six priority sections. You must decide how much of your income should go into each. It could look something like this: tithing takes up 10 percent of your income, expenses 10 percent, spending 25 percent, taxes 35 percent. When you budget, 100 percent of your outgo is accounted for. Get the idea? Let's look at six big budget areas. Here's what your budget looks like while you're still living at home.

(1) *Tithing—10 percent.* Your tithe should be taken right off the top. Remember, firstfruits go to God. Before you spend any of your money, give your tithe to your church.

(2) *Spending—25 percent.* Everyone likes to spend money and that's OK. There are things that we need and want to purchase. Things wear out and need replacing, like clothes, bike parts, or shoes. It's good to have a plan or decide what you will spend your money on before you go out. But it's also good to spend a bit of money on entertainment or going out with friends. Wise spending is the key.

(3) *Long-Term Savings—10 percent.* Remember those big future goals that you are planning for? You'll need to save for college, or maybe for that car. A percentage of your income should go into saving for those long-term future needs.

(4) *Short-Term Savings—25 percent.* Let's not forget about putting money into those short-term savings goals (like a new bike).

Remember your short-term savings account is also the flexible hero of the unpredictable, so keep it strong by giving it a good dose of deposits as often as you can.

(5) *Taxes—5 percent.* This is what you might pay into the family coffers if your income is from allowances, gifts, etc. It goes toward fun things for the whole family. It's much less than you'll have to pay the government if you get a regular job. If you are old enough to be in the workplace, you will have to pay taxes. The government takes a percentage off your paycheck to pay for roads, government projects, and other things we take for granted. Your employer will take your taxes off your check for you. If you work for yourself, you need to look into the self-employment tax laws. Your parents can help you.

(6) *Expenses—25 percent or more.* What are expenses? They are the costs of living and doing stuff. If you're working, you may pay some room and board to your parents. If you do, it will help your parents out, and it will help you prepare for paying rent when you move out. Expenses may also include lessons, community center fees, your own telephone, and bus money. You get the idea. As your monthly expenses change, you will have to adjust your budget percentages. Work it out, and you may need to change your savings or spending percentage to cover the new expense adjustment.

If you can put a percentage of your monthly income to each one of those six areas, you are on the road to smart money management and good stewardship. Budgeting plans kind of grow with you. Check out this full-fledged adult plan:

(1) Tithe
(2) Housing
(3) Automobile
(4) Debts
(5) Clothing
(6) Medical Expenses
(7) School/Child Care
(8) Taxes
(9) Food
(10) Insurance
(11) Entertainment and Recreation
(12) Savings
(13) Miscellaneous
(14) Investments
(15) Unallocated Surplus

As you get older and closer to moving out on your own, you'll probably add a few of these categories to your budget. Keep budgeting and when the time comes, this full budget will be a breeze.

# CHAPTER
## 5

# Banking

# #28—Bank on It

# The Bank!

If money is one of the most used inventions in the world, then banks must be one of the most used businesses in the world. Most everybody has some kind of bank account. Banks are often viewed as large alien worlds. Everybody who uses a bank should know how they work.

The bank is like any other store, except they buy and sell *money*. The bank "buys" money from the suppliers (that's you) and sells that money to customers (that's businesses and individuals). They sell money by loaning it to others for a fee. The bank lends the money you deposit with them to others for more money than they are paying you to keep it in their bank. That's how they afford to pay your interest and still make a profit. Your commercial bank's prime interest rate is determined by the country's central banking system called the Federal Reserve Bank. Buying and selling is called borrowing and lending. Banks are constantly juggling money from person to person and place to place, lending money to people and companies and borrowing it from you. It's a very complex system with, seemingly, all the money balls in the air at once.

# One Dark Knight

Banking has been a progressive invention with many cultures adding to it. During medieval times, an order of knights called the Knights Templars began to safeguard valuables, grant loans, and arrange for the safe transfer of funds from one kingdom to another—kind of like ancient armored cars on horseback.

Later, in the Renaissance, great banking families in Italy brought the concept to the world in a big way. But still later, in the seventeenth century, English goldsmiths stored and kept people's gold safe. Just like in banks, gold owners could ask for their gold anytime they liked. Soon the goldsmiths began to loan gold for a fee. Paper or promissory notes were used to keep track of things. Does this sound familiar? There you have it! The start of banking as we know it today.

# Banks Today

The role of banks today is varied. The central bank (Federal Reserve) serves both the government and the country's banking community. The central bank handles the government's incoming and outgoing money, its government-to-government loans, and how much new money is printed. They also have the important job of governing commercial banking regulations. Most importantly, the central bank is a huge regulating body whose main focus is the public interest, not the nation's banks.

The banks that we see around our town are called commercial banks, savings and loans, and credit unions. What is the purpose of banking institutions for us ordinary people? Banks store, use, monitor, and increase our savings. They handle the flow of our money in and out of our accounts from checks and credit cards to electronic banking. Banks keep track of the up and down motion of our accounts. They provide a quick, easy readout (statement) of how much money we have in our accounts, and how much interest we are being paid or are paying. If used properly, banks are a very important tool for money management.

It's clear that busy banks do a lot for us on a daily transaction-by-transaction level. Is there more? Yes. Banks can invest in you and your dreams. Banks can give business counseling, help you organize your business money matters, loan you the money to start a business, and help you pay back that money in manageable monthly payments. Banks can be one of the number one investors in your career.

The important thing to remember is that banks don't want to see businesses or individuals fail. If you get financially over your head, the bank loses not only their money but future loans with you. Don't forget that a bank is a business. If you are unhappy with your present bank, you can change. Banks know this, so they work hard to keep you and your money as a valued customer. Banks can provide you with friendly investment guidance, debt counseling, good banking services, personal and business financial support, and a range of other important services.

# #29—Loans

# Working off Your Loan

Loans can be the start of dreams or, if misused, a weight around our necks. When we borrow money for things like cars, boats, or vacations, we're paying interest on things that are depreciating (going down) in value. The new car we wanted might be a junker before it's paid for. It's just so tempting to buy now and pay later. Borrowing money is borrowing from future paychecks. If you're not careful, you'll be working today for money you already spent years ago.

The Bible warns, *"The rich rule over the poor, and the borrower is servant to the lender"* (Proverbs 22:7). Before you borrow, remember these points:

(1) Never borrow needlessly.
(2) Make your first small loan ventures with your parents.
(3) Loans raise a price tag.
(4) Make the loan benefit your future, not take from it.
(5) Make sure your purchase will last longer than the loan.
(6) Always deal with banks with a solid history, fair interest rates, and clear loan policies.
(7) Pay back your loan on time or, even better, ahead of schedule.
(8) If you have trouble with your payments, contact your creditor (the person you owe) to find a workable solution.

The trick to loans is finding the right loan and interest rate. There are many types of loans. Loans are like a chest full of tools. You need exactly the right one to get the job done.

# Personal Loan

Personal loans are small loans the bank lends to individuals. Today, personal loans are often arranged for items like cars, boats, or computers. Personal loans are very tempting. It's easy to let our desire for things drive us to the bank. Stop. Loans equal more time at work. Saving for personal things is the smart way to go.

# Mortgage Loan

Mortgage loans are used when people want to purchase land or buildings. They have part of the money (down payment) but not all. The bank will send surveyors to check out what you want to buy.

They give the bank a report on what it's worth. The bank compares this report with your loan request, income, and other debts. The bankers need to know that you have enough available money each month to make the payments. The bank wants to make sure loaning you money is a safe business venture. If everything meets with the bank's approval, you can put up your "sold" sign.

## Collateral

The bank seems like a good deal. You want something—*flash, bang, zoom*—you have it. Caution: the bank isn't a wishing well. Banks need to know they can trust you and that you'll pay back your loan. Even with a sparkling history, they may want some insurance.

Collateral is one way they can get that. You provide information on other valuables you own, like property, jewelry, or savings bonds that will equal the balance of the money you're borrowing. If you cannot repay your loan, the bank takes your valuables. Those valuables are collateral for your loan.

## Co-Signing Loans

Having a third person co-sign your loan is like having a person as collateral. This third person has to have the financial resources to back your loan. If you can't repay your loan (because you bumped your head and lost your memory), the third person will provide the money or collateral to pay it for you.

Wait! If you need someone to co-sign a loan, you shouldn't have a loan! *"Do not be a man who strikes hands in pledge or puts up security for debts; if you lack the means to pay, your very bed will be snatched from under you"* (Proverbs 22:26–27).

## Payback Time

If you do have a loan, it's crucial to make your monthly loan payments (installments) on time. As Christians, we need to be honest and reliable in all our business and financial dealings. When we borrow, we're giving our word that we'll repay that money on time. Remember, loans were designed to help people in need—not provide things you really don't need. Be money smart about loans.

# #30—Accounts: A Working Relationship

RYAN'S FIRST ACCOUNT

# Accounts

Having a bank account is a partnership. Don't be afraid to compare banks, accounts, and interest rates. Shop around for the best deal. Your account should be an important tool to help you save your money, keep track of it, and gain better control over it. Using the right account for the right job is the first step to banking wisdom.

## Savings Account

Savings accounts are great because they help you save money. The bank not only pays you interest, it will also pay you compound interest. That's interest on your interest. It pays you to keep the interest paid you in the bank.

When you open a savings account, the bank will give you an account register. This will help you keep your deposits, withdrawals, and interest payments organized. The bank will also send your account information in the mail, regularly.

The important thing to remember about a savings account is that it's for saving. When you save, it helps you prepare for God's future plans and your financial needs along the way. *"In the house of the wise are stores of choice food and oil, but a foolish man devours all he has"* (Proverbs 21:20). Saving is smart! Saving now can make it possible to afford the really important things when you need them. Saving keeps you free from debt and free to choose where, when, and how you're going to spend your money.

Open different savings accounts for your different types of saving plans or keep a book that shows how much is being saved for each savings goal. One account or many, just remember, you should always have some type of savings account working for you.

## Long-Term Savings Account

When you put your money into a long-term savings account, it's like packing it into a slow, dependable family car. When you use a long-term account, plan to leave your money in there until you reach your big savings goals. The bank may want a substantial minimum deposit for these types of accounts:

(1) Registered Education Savings Plan
(2) Individual Retirement Account or Registered Retirement Savings Plan

(3) Home Owners Savings Plans

In addition to these, youth accounts are often designed for long-term saving goals. The bank likes it when you leave your money with them for a long time. Why? They can make plans for your money. In fact, the bank wants to reward you by giving you a higher interest rate. To get this reward, most long-term savings accounts require you to keep your money in the account for a certain period of time. Yes, it's a good deal all around. You get to deposit as much money as you like and make more money; and the bank gets to use your money for for a long time.

# "CDs" Certificates of Deposits

This type of savings is like your money leaving home for a while to go to work. Fortunately, it goes to work for you. When you save, the idea is to get the best interest for your dollar. CDs do just that. You and the bank agree on a certain amount of money for you to deposit. You shake hands on how long you will leave that money with them. Unlike other savings accounts, you must leave your money in for the agreed time. No taking money out or there are substantial penalties.

You could call this a guaranteed investment certificate. The bank guarantees that it will give you a good interest rate, keep your money safe, and give you back your money plus interest at the end of the agreed time period. You guarantee that you'll leave your money in the bank until the time period is up. The reward is a higher interest rate. This is an excellent way to help you save faster. No touching equals no temptation.

# Short-Term Savings Accounts

A short-term savings account is like a race car account. Your money is only resting there for a short time. New ski boots or CD player? That sounds like a job for a short-term savings account! These types of accounts require a lower starting deposit to make your savings start-up easier. Short-term accounts are less predictable for the bank. Consequently, banks pay a lower interest rate. Your money doesn't work quite so hard for you in this account. Don't use a short-term savings account for a long-term goal.

# #31—Checking Accounts

# Check It Out

The checking account is like a financial airport, with money flying in and out on a daily or hourly basis. You write a check or use your bank card and the bank takes money out of your account.

Checks not only promise money, they also give the payee permission to take that money out of your account. You're making a promise to someone else that you have the money in the bank to back up your written pledge. The important thing to remember is that people are putting their trust in you.

# Keeping Score

How do we cover our checks? We have to link our brilliant budgeting system and our awesome record-keeping skills with our wise check writing. We need to know exactly how much of our monthly income should go into our checking account and what expenses and purchases we'll cover with our checks. We do this by keeping an up-to-date record of the deposits in the account and the checks we've written. Sometimes our checks come with carbon copies, check stubs, or a transaction register to help us keep track. Record the *balance*, the amount of money you have presently in your account. When you write a check, record the date, check number, the person you wrote it to, and the amount. Always subtract the check amount from your balance and record the new balance. Your checking account balance should never go below zero. Checks will start bouncing back to you instead of getting paid to the people waiting for your money, and you pay penalties.

You're doing your thing by writing checks and keeping track of your transactions and account balance. The bank is doing its thing by keeping track of the transactions that zip through your account. You get your checking account statement from the bank. Everything comes to a screeching halt. You and the bank disagree on the amounts in your account. How do you solve this difference?

You do something called reconciling with the bank. This helps you find out why there is a difference in your figuring. There are lots of reasons for account disagreements.

(1) *Error.* It's easy to make a math error. Maybe you forgot to write down a check. Maybe the bank made a mistake.
(2) *Charges.* Maybe some bank charges slipped through without

you recording them. Banks often charge a fee for keeping a checking account, writing checks, buying new designer checks, and bouncing a check.

(3) *The Float.* You may have written a check and recorded it, but the payee may not have cashed it yet. That check is floating around in an unknown spot in the system.

# Under Investigation

Spotting the source of differences is pretty easy, and it doesn't take an army of investigators. There's a form on the back of your account statement to use for reconciling your account. Be sure to follow the directions and do it every month. Here are three detective steps to snooping out the problem.

(1) *Compare Checks.* Determine which checks have been cashed. Place a mark in your checkbook beside each check number that's listed on your bank statement. If check 007 is listed in both your and the bank's records, it's been cashed.

(2) *Compare Deposits and Withdrawals.* Does your checkbook match the bank's account statement? If so, carry on.

(3) *Record the Unexpected.* After having double-checked both records you might find some lone riders in the group. If you have a few unmarked transactions that are only listed in one record, you may have found the problem.You forgot to record a deposit, withdrawal, check, or bank fee. Write down in your records and mark it off on the statement. Mystery solved.

# Cover Your Tracks

What happens if for some reason (like your dog ate your check register) you do write a "bad" check? Besides the fact that everybody looks at you funny, a bounced check is expensive. The bank charges you a fee for a bounced check, and most businesses charge you another one. In fact, that business may refuse to accept any more checks from you.

With careful account management you can stay on top of your transactions and finances. Learn to do it right from the start, and keep in the habit. Doing it right takes a lot less effort than cleaning up rubber check fallout.

# #32—Managing Your Savings

# Can You Manage?

The most important part of managing your savings account is managing to put money aside for it. Just like a checking account, you have to reconcile your savings account with your bank's statement. If you can navigate the rapids of a checking account, you have more than enough experience to tackle the quiet waters of your savings account. The saving process is simple. You regularly put aside a certain percentage of your income in your savings account. Sounds easy, but watch out for bad weather. The storm in your savings lake is, of course, temptation. Don't overspend for one savings goal and take from another.

It is so easy to put off your savings deposits. You see new sport shoes or a coat you really want. You decide to just skip this one week's or month's savings deposit to buy your stuff. You promise yourself that you'll deposit double next time. The world is full of things we want. Next time comes and goes with no deposit. Each month you have a new reason not to save. Your account becomes pretty stagnant. No money goes to work in your account.

# Wise Up

For your savings plan to be successful, you have to be committed to saving for the future. What's in your future? Remember your life map? Well, God's got a lot of exciting stops along the way, so save for them now! Sure, saving is for the important stops like college, but it is also for the "just fun" stops. When you save, you can have worry-free fun. When you know you can afford that movie or that day at the amusement park, you will enjoy it a whole lot more! When you work hard at saving, you should be able to play hard, too.

Your bank, parents, teachers, and friends cannot force you to save. You have to force yourself to save. Once you make that step, you will be surprised at how quickly your account will grow. It doesn't take much money each week before you notice a big difference. The more you save, the more it encourages you to save. You want to be committed, but how? There are lots of people in your life that will give you advice and help you get started. Go ask for advice.

Banks want to encourage new and younger clients. Many banks today have banking programs designed for children, teens, and their parents. They have teen programs and booklets designed for the beginner banker. They may also give out gifts as incentives. Most importantly, many junior savings accounts have a lower first deposit minimum, and a higher interest rate to encourage younger clients. Teen programs might include information on different account options, computer banking, and investment plans. Managing your savings account is making sure your money is in the right account and you are getting a good interest rate. That means consistent monthly tracking of all your long-term and short-term accounts.

A successful money management system is one that has three accounts helping you use, save, and make money. A checking account is for daily money matters. A short-term savings account is for little monthly needs. You don't need a whole lot of money in a short-term savings account. A long-term savings account or, even better, a CD, is a good account to transfer the bulk of your savings to, so you get the rewards of a higher interest rate.

Decide how much of your monthly income you wish to deposit in each account. It may take some time with pencil and paper, but with a little guidance you can put together a pretty impressive savings plan. Savings accounts aren't really that mysterious. They're just tools that can help you plan for your financial future. Set some goals and go after them by becoming savings savvy.

# #33—Cards

# Swipe Hype

Plastic cards with metal strips and computer codes have become the latest invention to make money management faster, easier, and more accurate. Every type of transaction has a card to match. We have debit cards, credit cards, gas cards, dining cards, store cards. . . . Let's take a look at two basic cards in our lives.

# Debit Card

Think of a debit card as a robobank packaged in a slick, super suit of plastic, computer-compatible and laser-technology fast. These debit cards are called ATM (Automated Teller Machine) cards, Insta-bank cards, or convenience cards. They have amazing powers.

They have the ability to connect you with your account any time you want. Most bank machines are linked into a system that lets you use them all. They are in malls, airports, stores, gas stations, and on campuses. Just slip your debit card in and you can do all your banking from anywhere, anytime. You can transfer funds, deposit or withdraw money, pay bills, do credit card payments, and get account statements. All at a speed never seen before.

Your card can even replace money and checks. Stores around the country are hooking up to the computer superhighway. When you want to buy something, you just pass the retailer your card—*swipe, swish, zoom*—they contact your bank's computer. You punch in your secret code, and flash! If you have that amount in your account, it automatically takes it out. The card is fast, convenient, useful, timesaving, hassle free, and eliminates floating checks. It is information at your fingertips! Great, right?

# Think Before You Link

This new freedom comes with a warning. There may be user fees attached. Don't let easy access mean spending excess. A debit card is just another useful banking tool as long as you don't let it change the way your most important tool thinks. Use your brain and consult your budget to decide when to use or not use your bank card. Keep careful records, and remember to keep your receipts so you can reconcile your statement.

# Careful! Credit Cards on Board

They're having fun! They dress right, laugh a lot, go where you've only dreamed of, and have the ticket to get there. That ticket is a credit card. How exciting, how now, how happening! Everybody seems to want you to have a credit card.

Like many things in life, that ticket has a hidden price. Credit cards can fool you into thinking they're just like money—but they aren't. When you use a credit card, you're *borrowing* money. Just like the banks, the credit card companies charge you for renting their money. Their fee or interest rate is very high! It doesn't take a whole lot of credit card use before you have one steep loan with a very high interest payment that gets bigger every week you don't pay it back. The Bible cautions us, *"The rich rule over the poor, and the borrower is servant to the lender"* (Proverbs 22:7). Credit companies can demand payment in other forms like lawsuits, repossessing items, or taking money straight from your paychecks. Credit card debt can haunt you and damage your credit rating.

# The Trick to Credit Cards

Like any financial tool, credit cards must be used properly. Here are some credit card pointers:

(1) Shop for a card with no annual fee.
(2) Only use your credit card if you have the money in your budget.
(3) Pay off your credit card bill in full each month!
(4) Keep careful records of all your credit card transactions, and reconcile your statement each month.
(5) Keep your card safe from theft.
(6) Choose a card that earns travel points or even cash back.
(7) Wise credit use can help you establish a good credit history.

The heart of the credit card problem isn't the card or the system. It's how we use the system. If we use our money and budgeting smarts, credit cards are useful tools. Credit only turns into debt when we mismanage our finances. In fact, a good credit rating speaks for our responsibility, management skills, and ability to use money wisely. Good credit can be good for our future.

So, credit isn't the enemy people think. Poor money stewardship is giving credit a bad name.

# #34—Digital Banking

# Wired Banking

What's digital banking? It's the banking of the future starting today. Digital banking is banking where we live. Banks and their computers are linked to our phone lines to enter our homes. Banking hours? What are banking hours? We can access our account information anytime we want from anywhere. No more teller lines, bank machines, or "the check's in the mail." This is straight, direct, telephone or computer-enhanced financial communication! Digital banking is coming to a home near you.

# Dial B for Banking

First, you can do all your banking by phone. Phone banking is great for the computerless. Like your bank card, you are given an account code that only you know. That code gives you phone access to your accounts. What can you do by phone? You can get account information, pay bills, transfer funds, arrange loans, manage your credit card, arrange a mortgage, set up term deposits, check interest rates, and receive bank information. That's some phone call!

How do you use your telephone to bank? After phoning your banking service, you are taken through the system by a friendly recorded voice. Each transaction you do is repeated back to you for confirmation. You can then change your instructions if they are incorrect. All your phone transactions will be recorded in your account statement immediately. Don't forget to record your transaction in your register. Do you feel funny talking to a recording? The phone bank assures us that we can speak to a real person anytime we wish. Whew, just when we thought nobody was really out there!

# bank@now.com

Second, you can bank by computer. The computer, one of man's most amazing inventions, has given a silicon boost to the old money invention. What business, classroom, or individual isn't linked to the net, or at least been on the net? The ranks of the unnetted are growing smaller every day. The net communicates to you, connects you, educates you, and promotes you. The net is condensed, packaged information zapped into your very lap (laptop that is).

The bank has caught the computer wave and is surfing the line for customers. Go to any bank today and you can pick up a pamphlet on computer banking. To get on the banking net, you need a computer with Internet access. The software can be ordered from your bank, often for free. Many banks don't charge an activation fee or a monthly access fee. Just boot, click, type, and you're into your secure banking link.

What can you do on the banking line? Let's download the list: access account statements, pay bills, transfer funds, manage your credit card, arrange your mortgage and loans, check interest rates, buy certificates of deposit, stop payments, find out about medical and travel insurance, buy or sell stocks, get financial news, and last but not least, obtain bank information. Wow, let's see a teller do all that in the click of a button!

## Upgrade?

Computer banking is here to stay. The power of the personal computer is lending a new type of power to banks. The interactive face of the computer is the future teller we'll click on. It's hard to say what the impact of this isolated but connected society will be. Is it just another step in the innovation that started thousands of years ago?

Use this new tool just as wisely as before and with God's guidance. Just remember, God doesn't have an e-mail address. Call Him direct.

## Call of the Times

Phone and computer banking are just a sign of the times. We don't want to waste a minute in our day-to-day lives. Our employers can direct deposit our checks into our accounts, we can shop at home on the net, we can have our office or classes at our home computer. We basically can run most our lives from one room. We don't have to meet anybody, see anybody, or apparently, hear anybody. Sure, it's convenient, fast, and modern. But, once in a while, it's nice to get out and be with flesh and blood. If we can eventually do everything without leaving home, remember to go out and mingle anyway.

# CHAPTER
## 6

# Spending

# #35—What Is Spending?

# Spending Sphere

Spending our money is in style big-time. And why not? There is a world out there full of things we can spend money on. But let's not get crazy about it. Spending is not, as you might think, the opposite of saving. Saving, as you already heard, is delayed spending. Spending is the process of using our money, and saving is part of spending our money *wisely*. Spending is simply exchanging our goods for another's. It's taking what we produced or earned and trading it for something we need. Spending is the way a community interacts and exchanges its gifts. Spending creates a sphere of contacts with other people.

Let's pretend you are a farmer. Not only are you a farmer, but you're a wealthy farmer. What do you do with all that wealth? Do you keep your money locked up forever? Why have it then? Remember, saving is part of spending wisely. We save so we can use our money for future plans. Dusty money is just dusty paper until it is used.

What's the right thing to do? If God has blessed you with prosperity, you can spread that prosperity by saving wisely and spending your money on family, giving people jobs, investing in your brother's new business, buying your neighbor's cow, giving to charities, or donating to your community. Spend your money to support your community and the people in it. Spending your money in your community helps make it prosper and grow. You buy shoes from the store. The store owner hires an employee to help in the store. That employee is your friend. Your friend earns money. The spending system is a chain that connects us and makes our community stronger. God is pleased when we spend our money on worthy things. *"Be rich in good deeds . . . be generous and willing to share"* (1 Timothy 6:18). Doing things with your money is not a selfish thing, it can be a helpful thing. Saving isn't just piling up money, it's planned and smart spending. With smart spending, you have the opportunity to touch your community.

# Spending Secret Service

Spending, like everything, has its special missions.

(1) We spend to provide for our daily necessities. We all need the basics to live: shelter, food, and clothing.

(2) We spend to experience different things and to enjoy life. There's nothing wrong with spending on ourselves and spending to have fun. Just remember, like a balanced diet, we have to have a balanced spending plan.

(3) We spend to educate ourselves or start a business. Investing in ourselves or others is part of following God's plan for us and part of being in a community.

(4) We spend to give. Tithing and charity is the real secret service of our spending plan. Giving to others makes us and our spending special. When we give, we should do it for the joy of giving, not to show off.

*"Be careful not to do your acts of righteousness before men, to be seen by them. If you do, you will have no reward from your Father in heaven. So when you give to the needy, do not announce it with trumpets, as the hypocrites do in the synagogues and on the streets, to be honored by men. I tell you the truth, they have received their reward in full. But when you give to the needy, do not let your left hand know what your right hand is doing, so that your giving may be in secret. Then your Father, who sees what is done in secret, will reward you"* (Matthew 6:1–4). Remember, not only is spending on others important, but so is our attitude.

When we have a spending plan, we know how much money we can put into each spending mission. As good stewards, we are listening to God's direction for our giving. When we spend wisely, we are saving for now and the future every day. When we spend with a God-based plan, we are a light to the world by showing our community the godly way of handling money. People will wonder why we aren't in debt. Then we can introduce them to our Financial Advisor. After all, God's office is open all day!

# #36—Consumer Industry

# Dazzle

Allure, dazzle, style, glamour—these are more than just words. They are illusions. What do I mean by that? These things appear to be spectacular, but are actually ordinary. That's the trick of advertising—it makes ordinary things seem extraordinary. The advertisers present their products in ways that will appeal to us. Food, clothes, cars, vacations, and even toilet bowl cleaners are packaged to look incredible! The advertisers want us to *want* to buy their products.

Advertising companies are the masters of trend. They have spent years learning exactly what catches our attention and what appeals to us. Advertising is part art, part science, part illusion, part showmanship, and sometimes even part truth. From the man who shouts, "Step right up!" at the fair to the billion dollar soft drink commercials, they make us stop and stare and, most importantly, buy. They use an entire stockpile of advertising tools: television, magazines, movies, and billboards. You name it, they'll use it to attract an audience. Advertising works because it spends billions every day to make us spend billions and billions—each and every one of us.

# Fast Moves

We live in a consumer-motivated society. Our country's economy is built on buying things or services. Consumers equal products equal buyers equal profits equal employees equal consumers. If people stopped buying, stores would close, companies would stop manufacturing, and people would be out of jobs. It's an endless cycle of supply and demand. To keep that buying level high, companies hire professionals to make their products desirable. From icy-looking soft drinks to sleek automobiles (complete with tuxedo-clad drivers). They want you to wonder, "How could I survive without that product?" They want you to think, "Wow! Trendy, glamourous, alluring, stylish, and dazzling or, at the very least, useful!" Advertisers will go to pretty wild lengths to separate you from your money. It's a job, and we love the commercials, don't we! They're fun. But don't forget, they are just an informational tool, not a lifestyle.

# Sales Pitch

Just one television station may run hundreds of commercials each day. Advertisers employ thousands of people whose sole purpose in business is to get you to spend your money on their stuff. Their concern is product sale, not your financial welfare.

Do you feel outnumbered? You may be, but, when you educate yourself about how advertising and marketing work, you will be able to see through the hype. Your greatest tool is cerebral spending and brain budgeting. God has given you the tools to do both. Be a consumer who is content, calm, cool, and collected. That means ignoring the hype and focusing on what you really need, want, and can afford. Here's some advertising advice.

(1) Decide for yourself what you need by listening closely to what the advertiser is saying. Write a list of other things you could buy with the same money. Would you really put that product on the top of the list?

(2) Compare products. Don't just buy what is advertised.

(3) Shop around. Don't just go where the commercials tell you to.

(4) Go for quality. Make sure the product lives up to its advertiser's claim. Look for good quality.

(5) Look past the appeal of looking good or cool. What can that product really do for you?

## *Soon Parted*

Part of becoming a smart consumer is thinking before you part with your money. How many times have you bought something and been disappointed later when it didn't look anything like the advertisement? Your burger wasn't quite so big and juicy looking. Your model airplane doesn't really fly. Be aware and compare before you buy anything! Become a consumer snoop. Find out if you got what you were promised! If not, return it.

Before you buy, be sure you understand the return policies. Educate yourself on your rights as a consumer and be prepared to insist on them. If your purchase is not what it should be, you have several options.

(1) Take it back for a replacement or a refund.

(2) Ask the company to repair the problem for free until you are satisfied with the product.

(3) Contact consumer protection agencies or the Better Business Bureau. Make both manufacturers and advertisers live up to the "look" they created. You can be an impulse-buying buster by being aware of marketing magic and having a spending plan.

# #37—Spending Plan

# Perfect Plan

We talked about all kinds of plans: God's plan, our plan, a savings plan, and planning for success. Now, what exactly is a spending plan? Before we spend our money, we should have a very good idea where it will be going. Stores can be a maze of products, advertisements, salespeople, temptation, and peer pressure. If you don't have a spending plan and the resolve to stick to it, then avoiding the pitfalls of that maze isn't easy! While our savings plan is the filter that helps us avoid all that confusion, our spending plan is a ladder over the maze wall. Go straight for what you need, not what you might want. When you stick to your spending plan, it is like sticking to your life plan. It accomplishes what God wants. Remember, there is nothing wrong with window shopping and even deciding on something you would like to buy. The key is not to buy it *then*. Go work it into your plan. Sticking to your spending plan may mean hard choices, but it can be done. It's all a matter of intent and timing.

# Intent

Have you heard the term "the intent to commit a crime"? That means you have a plan to do something not so nice. You should have the intent to commit a wise buy. Plan to do some smart shopping. Intent is all about will, and willpower is your decision to stick by your earlier decisions. Say you decided to go out and buy new jeans. Your intent is to buy only those jeans. You have money in your pocket, ready to shop. Remember—only buy that pair of jeans!

You hit the stores with the intention of just buying that pair of jeans still strong. But (there is always a but), you found some shirts on sale that look great with the jeans, and those new loafers would be nice, too. You go home with your new jeans and an armful of other stuff. Your willpower bit the dust. Your spending plan was in order, your intent was right, but you kind of lost control there towards the end.

Here's how to stay a little more in control. Take a little mad money. Buy your jeans first, then switch gears. Now go spend your mad money on something fun! Buy a small treat or go to a good movie. Being a wise shopper doesn't mean we can't be spontaneous with a certain amount of our money. We just have to know the limits of our budget. Our budget is not meant to be a spending straitjacket. It's meant to be a guide to our spending adventures!

# Time

Timing is everything in shopping control. Is this the right time for your purchase? Do you really need it right now? Can you afford it right now? Is this the best time to buy? Can you get a better deal at another time like buying ice skates in summer or camping equipment in winter?

Plan for your spending by choosing when you go. Don't go grocery shopping on an empty stomach. Don't go shopping when you are way too tired and stressed out. When you are tired, you can't focus on smart comparison shopping. You just buy to get out of the store. Don't go with a friend who has a history of talking you into buying sprees. Go shopping when you feel in control and ready to do some consumer snooping.

# My Plan!

You have control when it comes to when you shop, how you shop, and where you shop. Maximize your control by being organized, shopping comparatively, having clear shopping lists, a cash limit, and consumer marketing savvy. Shopping smart isn't hard! You have already been learning good stewardship methods and life planning skills. Apply those to your spending savvy. You just need willpower, organization, and a "pay now for now" attitude. It just means sticking to the plan. Shopping is actually a lot more fun this way. You're in control, not the stores, and it feels great when you know that you have a plan and you've stuck to it!

# #38—Wise Buys

# Wise Up

Marketing makeovers make buying look better than it is. The problem with marketing makeovers is that the products aren't nearly as tempting once we know what they look like underneath all the dressing. When we learn about the facts behind marketing, we may not be so quick to spend. What's a wise buy? It's getting the best value for your money. First, pray for consumer wisdom and a fair deal. Check out all your consumer corners.

Remember, buying and selling is a relationship. Both sides have to care about the needs of the other. We don't want a good deal that's not good for the seller. A fair deal comes from consumer knowledge and an understanding of the needs of the market. Both are important. A good buy is one that is fair to you and supports the businesses in your community.

# Big Discount

This is the most common sales surprise. Let's call this "the disappearing money act." Sellers like to do fancy moves with their prices. The price is basically how much it will cost you to buy. If the price is too high, you won't buy. If the price is too low, the manufacturers or retailers won't be able to cover their production and store costs.

Manufacturers sell their products to a store and give a suggested retail price that will make the store a profit. Let's say the company suggests the stereo store sells its new CD players for $100. The store doesn't have to sell it for a $100. It can sell it for more, say $150. That's fifty dollars more than even the manufacturer said it was worth. When we shop we should be aware that we could be paying more than we should. Even if the store lowers its already high price to, say, $112, is that a discount? Sad to say, it isn't. The lesson here is to ignore the big signs that declare "On Sale" or "Big Deals." They just look like big savings. Instead go out there and really shop. Compare prices!

# Fast Moves

Like magicians rely on the hand being quicker than the eye, stores rely on the want being faster than the brain. "Impulse buying" is buying something before you have a chance to really think about it. Stores promote impulse buying big-time. The supermarket puts chocolate bars and magazines by the checkout for you to grab just before you leave. *Abracadabra*—it's in your bag and on its way home. There are ways to avoid impulse buying. For instance, take only enough money for the things you need. If you want to buy something unexpectedly, wait a day or two, then see if you can put it in your plan. If you feel pressured by a salesperson, walk away and get some air. Come back another day. Take a friend with you who is also managing his or her money properly. It helps to have a good shopping team that encourages each other's spending plan. Remember, don't say, "No," say, "Plan!"

The "one time only" sale is another trick. You are only given one opportunity to buy at this great "one day only" low price. Usually there are only a few of the items left to add to the pressure. There is something about shoppers that love to beat the consumer clock or grab the very last one. Why play the game? Stop if the item isn't part of your plan. Leave the store and come back another day.

# Invisible Savings

That's right, it is invisible because the savings aren't really there. Sellers sometimes try to convince buyers that they are saving money when they buy. Think about it. I mean, really think about it. How can you save money when you are already spending money? You can't spend and save at the same time. Impossible! You may be getting a small discount but you are definitely not saving. Spending is not saving.

# Going Behind the Counter

Going behind the counter of the selling business is an eye-opener. Sometimes the only way to understand marketing makeovers is to slow down and really look. Don't be distracted by other things. Just focus on what you really need. When we slow down, we can shop and compare. Wise shopping is educated, controlled, and backed by knowledgeable consumer action. When we shop, we want to act responsibly, not react impulsively. Smart consumer shopping is a balance that makes both sides happy. We want to get good buys, but we also want the seller to make a fair living. When both sides are open and honest with each other, that is the best deal of all.

# #39—Debt and Credit

# Debt Department

How come everybody seems to be lining up in front of the Debt department? Is there a sale on again? Debt hasn't always been housed in such a big building. Our country has added a brick to it year after year until we've made a pretty impressive monument to overspending.

There are countless highly-paid professionals in all walks of life that have found their financial ground sinking fast. Why? Because they did not apply basic money management to their lives. They didn't learn about budgeting, saving, spending wisely, good investments, and a God-based outlook on money matters. Talk to many actors, athletes, musicians, and others, and they will tell you they earned too much money, too fast, too soon. They had trained for their careers, but not how to handle their financial success. Nobody told them how to handle money, so while they made big money, they ended up in even bigger debt.

How did we get over our financial heads? We took a very fast ride on the speedboat called *over-borrowing*. Funny name for a boat. Funny way to manage our money and our country. I grant you, over-borrowing was a great ride while it lasted. We got to cruise in style.

Let's say the water is your annual income. It keeps you afloat. A strange thing happens when you take that over-borrowing boat ride. The longer you stay in that boat, the heavier it gets. Soon it begins to sink into your income until your income just can't support the weight of your demands any longer. When that happens, my friend, you are sunk. You are over your head and going down fast. You may be able to tread water for a little while. People sometimes manage to extend their credit. That means you borrow more money to pay off the money you already borrowed and spent. Still sinking and going down fast! If you can't pay off one debt, how is borrowing more going to help? Extending your credit past what your income can afford drags you under the crashing waves of debt.

The credit system is not the problem. Remember, credit is not debt. The credit system is just like a boat, it can be used responsibly or recklessly. When we use credit, we should follow these safety rules:

(1) Back your credit use with money you have saved already.
(2) Pay all your credit card payments completely each and every month.
(3) The first time you can't pay off your credit card bill, retire your credit card to the back bench of your financial plan. Cut it up. Whatever it takes.
(4) Use your credit as a tool to enhance your money management, not to increase your spending power. Never use credit as a replacement for money you don't have.

## God's View on Debt

What is God's view on debt? *"The wicked borrow and do not repay, but the righteous give generously"* (Psalm 37:21). In the Bible, borrowing and lending were not used as a way to finance life. It was used as a way to help the poor. The way debt is viewed today is the reverse of God's system. We want things now and hope we can pay for them later. When we look for quick fixes and schemes, the water starts filling the boat. Watch out! When we start to accumulate debt, we have cast off the lines, and we've left God's dock. If we want to stay near the financial shore, we have to trust God to teach us how to approach our financial problems in a different light. God wants us to solve our money matters before we start sinking. How? By seeking God, trusting His Word, and taking advice from godly people with financial experience.

## Money

There is nothing wrong with spending and enjoying money as long as we are following God's financial principles. The younger we learn this, the easier our financial boat ride is going to be. We can be righteous in the way we handle money matters. Everything in our lives, including loans and investments, must have a godly foundation to work properly. When we hear water lapping, let's reach for God's help first. We'll breathe easier when we do.

# #40—Giving Wisely

# Giving Graciously

Why do we give? Our God is a giving God. If He's our example, shouldn't we be giving people? We have faith in God's love for us and His desire to provide for us. He wants us to share His generosity with others. It's all part of His plan. *"You will be made rich in every way so that you can be generous on every occasion, and through us your generosity will result in thanksgiving to God"* (2 Corinthians 9:11). When we give with a joyful heart, we help others experience God's love and caring. Giving is saying thank-you to God for what He has done in our own lives. Pass God's generosity on!

Giving should be both focused and effective. You can have a giving heart and still not accomplish much. Let's say you're in a big giving mood. You go to the top of a tall building with two boxes. One is full of Bibles and one is full of money. First you throw the Bibles down to the street. Well, people are getting the message all right! They're running for cover. Bibles are making a smashing impression on their lives. Is this an effective ministry? Nope. Next you throw money down. People need money, right? Don't look now, but people are scrambling to catch the fluttering bills. Cars are screeching to a halt. People are fighting.

So you see, giving has to be planned and purposeful. We don't necessarily give to every ministry or everyone who asks us. How do we know the who, where, what, and how of giving?

(1) Tithe at your local church.
(2) Pray about what mission projects to donate to.
(3) Ask your parents or pastor about charity organizations.
(4) Volunteer at your community or church charity.
(5) Fill in where you see a need. Reading to the elderly, helping with charity sports, or baby-sitting to free up adults to go to meetings are all possibilities. Talk to your minister about mission support ideas. Remember, once you start, be committed.

# Not So Far Away

(Adapted from Matthew 25:31–46)

When we think about mission work, we think of doctors in deep Amazonian jungles or Bible translators in huts in Africa. Actually, mission work can be found right in our backyard.

God sees when we take the time to take care of the needs of others. *"Come, you who are blessed by my Father; take your inheritance, the kingdom prepared for you since the creation of the world. For I was hungry and you gave me something to eat."* Seeing the needs of others requires keeping our eyes open. Don't have a giving heart only at Christmas or the church charity picnic. Let it be part of your everyday life—like giving your sister and her friends the last cookies.

*"I was thirsty and you gave me something to drink."* Let's follow Jesus' example. He was great at giving. We could get our whole family involved and, for instance, give a food hamper full of everyday things to a family having tough times.

*"I was a stranger and you invited me in."* We can let giving to others be as impersonal as writing a check, or we can do it in a personal way. We could baby-sit for a single mom without charging or host a youth group exchange weekend.

*"I needed clothes and you clothed me."* Look at your prosperity and think of ways to share it. Sponsor a child overseas or take clothes and toys to a shelter to brighten a needy mother's day.

*"I was sick and you looked after me."* Keep your hearts compassionate for the weak in spirit and health. Look into volunteering at your local hospital, nursing home, or church or community charity.

*"I was in prison and you came to visit me."* Show a loving heart to those who may not know the right path. If the lonely bully down the street steals your football, forgive him. If he won't return the ball, pray about it. Maybe God wants you to give it to him and tell him why.

# *Wow!*

When we do these things the King will say, *"I tell you the truth, whatever you did for one of the least of these brothers of mine, you did for me."* Giving wisely is about more than just separating your charity money from the rest of your income. It's more than writing a check. Giving wisely is about your heart and the way you live your life. A good place to start is in your home and neighborhood. If you won't do it there, the rest is just a show. A giving attitude will make its way into every area of your life. It's about treating people like you would treat the King. Giving is about more than money matters. It's also about heart matters.

# #41—Rock the World

# Loud and Clear

Have you ever taken music to the beach with you? You set up your spot, drop your towel, and turn up the sound. Everybody around you can hear your music. From the type of music you play, people are forming an opinion about you. Your music is saying a lot about what's inside you. The lyrics to the music tell people what you think is right or moral—what your values are. You're making a statement by the music you choose to listen to.

That goes for how you spend your money, too. Remember, every time you buy something, you're making a statement of approval. You are, and so are your friends. You can change the world with how you spend your money. Even if you're not old enough to legally vote, you've got voting power where it counts. Who's counting those votes? The retail market, the entertainment industry, and the service industry all watch carefully what you buy and why. They employ thousands of people to study your buying habits, what type of products attract you now, and what will attract you in the future. Just as in real-life politics, these people need your vote to stay in office or at least in business.

A survey in 1993 on teens stated that 28.5 million teens in the United States spent $28 billion and influenced another $155 billion in family spending in one year. This trend is skyrocketing us into the year 2000. Those are money matters that companies take seriously. Companies know that the shopping malls are the place to be for teenagers. Teens usually spend between $10 and $50 per visit. The average teen makes three trips to the mall per month. That adds up!

If you think what you do doesn't really matter, you are so wrong! It does matter! Are you waiting for God to use you to make a difference? Stop waiting. He can use you right now and right where you are. *"Don't let anyone look down on you because you are young, but set an example for the believers in speech, in life, in love, in faith and in purity"* (1 Timothy 4:12).

What companies and products you reelect is up to you. Ignore the flashy campaigns and big-name promoters. Hold up those companies and products to what you know is right. Ask yourself, "From a Christian perspective, do they deserve my vote of approval?" The only person who can cast your vote is you. Your voting power is a matter of your money speaking up for what you feel is right. Next time you go to see or rent a movie or buy a book, make sure it's one that promotes God's values. When we don't buy or rent a video that, say, promotes violence, we're telling the producers not to make violent movies. When enough people don't buy a product, they shout to the world what they believe. We can, and do, change the world. Remember, companies are watching exactly what you and your friends buy. Focus in on what *you* think about a product. If you think it's wrong to support a group financially because of their lyrics, then you probably shouldn't be listening to their music in the first place. Go with your conscience. Go a step further and write the company to explain why you won't buy their product.

Consumer selection has changed the world. It has influenced governments and entire worldviews. Consumer campaigns have changed the way we think about things. We can harness our buying power to promote godly missions and change the world.

## *Around the World to Your Back Door*

Don't think that your financial influence is restricted to global views. You can also use your money to support local businesses that promote good values and have good services or products. Wouldn't it be a good idea to show you care by doing business with people who care about the right things? When you support someone in your community, you can see right away how your money touches lives.

As Christians, we can use that consumer power to effect positive change. When you buy good stuff, you're contributing to what's good. Voting with your wallet is using God's money for His purposes. Remember, you're just managing it for Him. Go out there and make each of God's dollars work for the most good. That's like turning up the sound so everybody can hear God more clearly!

# Career

# #42—Career Line

# What's My Line?

What is a career? It should be more than a vague idea of something you're going to do to make money. A career is a life goal that we attain by working through a number of smaller personal, educational, or business achievements. When we think about what type of career we want, we have to sit down, pray, and ask God for His plan for us. Remember, God is our career counselor.

# Long Distance Phone Call?

We are not alone when it comes to our personal career planning. God wants to be there for us. He wants to give us direction and wisdom when it comes to career relationships, decisions, and challenges that we encounter. He wants to open doors and opportunities. God wants to do a lot of things for us. What does He want from us? He wants us to want Him. Let's not make God wait for us in the want ads. Let's go to Him first before we make our career choices. God is calling, so pick up the phone!

# Getting the Message?

God has called us to a ministry. God doesn't call just ministers and missionaries to a career that serves Him. There are no teacher's pets when it comes to God. He has a career plan for everybody, not just the brainy kid in the back row of your math class, or the school's star football player. If you are following God's life map for you, you are following His overall plan for His kingdom!

People may think God has pet careers. He doesn't. God values every aspect of His church, from the child selling lemonade to the preacher in His pulpit. We don't have to be working in careers that are directly connected to the church. Any career that has God's blessing and direction is a job that is working for Him.

God has the perfect job waiting for us. He has planned every aspect of it—the achievements, training, preparation along the way, and the joy of doing that job. He has placed talents, events, opportunities, and people in our lives to help us discover the career He designed especially for us. Have faith that the way He made you perfectly matches what He planned for you to do.

# Disconnected

If God has a career plan for everybody, why are there so many completely misplaced and unhappy people? Good question. There are many reasons why so many people are disconnected from God, and dissatisfied with their jobs. Maybe we're just not listening to God. He's calling, but we're not picking up the phone. Maybe we are letting other messages break into our line with God. Are money issues, possessions, other people's ideas, and a desire for power causing static with your connection to God's will? God doesn't want to shout over static. God also doesn't want to discuss our career on a party line connected to selfish desires, money, and all those other party guys. *"You shall have no other gods before me"* (Exodus 20:3).

Are you putting God on hold? Worse yet, are you listening to your call-waiting while talking with God? Do you think other messages in your life are more important? Is God leaving messages on your answering machine that you aren't returning? Your communication time with God should be direct, one-on-one, and the most important phone call of the day. God wants to quietly sit down with us and talk over His desire for our professional lives. God wants us to have jobs that make us happy and complete. Trust Him to do that! What we do with our lives fulfills God's plan for our world. We can all be part of that! God is giving us instructions on our careers if we just keep the phone line clear.

# Why Is God Calling?

We know that what the world values is not what God values. Many of the stories in the Bible are about the contrast between God's desire for the world and people's own desires. Ever since Adam and Eve, God has looked for and selected people to carry out His vision and to be role models for the world.

God wants us to join that long list of people in history that had hearts for Him. He wants us to uphold the things that He sees as worthy and desirable. The career He gives us and the godly path we follow all help build His kingdom. We may think, "Wow. God must be on His cellular phone to a lot of people every day." You're right. God's love isn't confined by any of the things that we see as limits. There is enough of Him to go around. God is watching and guiding you all the way. When you want to connect with God, do it. God's waiting to talk privately with you. Are you available?

# #43—Choices

# A Whale of a Choice!

From the moment you wake up you have choices to make. Every action you take is a choice. Instant little choices are choices you forget about an hour later. Let's call them Cheerios© or Captain Crunch© choices. Choices also come in the larger variety. There are times in your life when huge choices come to the surface. They are more the grab-the-whale-by-the-tail choices. They can change your future and the way you look at life. If you're not careful, they can even change your walk with God. When we encounter these big choices, how do we know which is the right one? Simple. The formula for career planning is to pray, plan, and keep praying as we go.

# Which Direction to Take?

How do we find out what God's plan is? Easy, just open the Book. We can look to the Bible for that answer. What examples are there? There are certain things that the great people in the Bible did when they wanted to hear from God.

(1) *Bible heroes knew the Word of God.* They gained a clear understanding of God's desire. Jesus knew the Scripture even when He was very young. *"After three days they found him in the temple courts, sitting among the teachers, listening to them and asking them questions. Everyone who heard him was amazed at his understanding and his answers"* (Luke 2:46–47). What is God's response to us? Jesus said, *"Whoever believes in me, as the Scripture has said, streams of living water will flow from within him"* (John 7:38). We read the Bible to learn how life works. The more we know about the instruction manual and the more we follow it, the better life will work.

(2) *Bible heroes actively looked for God.* They had a desire to talk with Him, seek His direction, and do things His way. What is God's response to us seeking Him? He seeks us! *"And without faith it is impossible to please God, because anyone who comes to him must believe that he exists and that he rewards those who earnestly seek him"* (Hebrews 11:6).

(3) *Bible heroes waited for God's timing.* Noah waited for the flood and the retreat of the water. What was God's response to his faith and patience? *"Then God blessed Noah and his sons,*

*saying to them, 'Be fruitful and increase in number and fill the earth' "*(Genesis 9:1).

(4) *Bible heroes were willing to do what God instructed.* Doubtful Moses was willing to do God's will in Egypt. What was God's response to him? *"Now go; I will help you speak and will teach you what to say"* (Exodus 4:12).

When we learn about God and seek Him out, when we trust in His timing and act on His instructions, we will find out what He wants from us. The closer we get to God, the closer we get to understanding our mission in life.

# *This Is It?*

Wait a minute! You've been listening to God, but the job you're in isn't getting you where you think God wants you. This job isn't even making you happy—it's just barely meeting your personal and financial needs. What's the deal? Remember to have faith in God's plan for you. Many Bible characters were doing completely different things when God stepped in and worked in their lives in a big way. David and Moses were shepherds. Joseph was sold as a slave by his brothers. How's that for a lower level career starter? Did their lives stop there? No, they listened and learned from God their whole lives.

All the stops along your life path are part of God's plan. What Joseph learned about himself and serving God, he learned both as a slave and a leader of men. Where you are now is not necessarily where you are going to be later in life. The point is to do your present job with all the enthusiasm and dedication that you can. Your attitude toward God and your career is your choice. How you deal with life's challenges is your choice. How you view your present situation is also your choice. Do you have a good attitude or a bad one? Just remember, God values all your works, great and small. Conduct your life like God is the boss—because He is.

# #44—You!

# Personality

You've got personality! It is completely unique and made up of the qualities that make you *you*. Your personality is the way you think, the way you behave, and the emotions you experience.

How do we get a personality? Science does know that many of our personality traits are there the moment we are born. Some babies are more active and others are calmer. Other personality characteristics develop as we begin to live with our families and experience life. Who we play with, the place we live, and our community all help influence our growing and changing personalities.

# It's So You!

Your personality is so you! Did you know that? And being you is the best thing you can be! Part of being the best *you* is learning how you work best. Learning about you is all about taking personal inventory. Learning more about your personality can help you find out what you are best suited for.

# Put It to the Test

Spend a day studying people in your school. Watch the way they behave and the things they do. They all have different personalities! Your personality is one of God's big clues to revealing what career is best suited to you. One of the ways to understand your personality is to assess it and find out what your personality strengths and weaknesses are.

Personality tests are only useful if you answer them honestly. The assessment won't change you, and for most people, the results aren't surprising. You probably already know what type of personality you have, but the assessment may suggest some careers that you hadn't considered before. Personality assessments are just a tool. Don't let them put you in a box, and remember—following God's plan is the number one priority.

# Get Results

After taking the assessment, you will discover your personality strengths and weaknesses. No personality is right or wrong, better or worse. They are just different. A personality assessment can show you how to maximize your strengths. Maybe you're great at talking with people, but you are also a little disorganized. So let's find a way to make your great communications skills work for you and to improve your organizational skills.

How can your career and personality work together? When you put together your life map, consider these things:

(1) *Your career choice should be something you like.* There is no point in pursuing a career that you hate doing. Part of excelling in a career is enjoying the work.

(2) *Your career choice should be something you feel comfortable doing.* You may be very creative and artistic, so you become a graphic designer for some successful magazine or ad company. Great, right? Wrong. You can't stand high pressure and tight deadlines. This job would only make you tense and uncomfortable.

(3) *Your career choice should be something you are good at.* Find out what skills and abilities are required in the career you're investigating. Are they ones you know you already have or ones you can successfully train for? Find out before you invest your time.

Career planning with God will help you avoid false starts. Your personality strengths that God gave you can make you the right person for the job. When that happens, watch out! Great things are sure to follow! God sure knows how to pull a gift together!

# *Gifting*

Talent? Talent is a special ability or gift to do something well. We've all heard talent buzz phrases: math whiz, superstar, green thumb, artistic eye, musical prodigy. . . They are words we use to describe people with particular gifts or talents. We all have talents (Romans 12:6–8). Some people discover their talents early in life. Many of us have to spend more time learning about how God created us before we truly understand what our talents are. That's OK. Don't panic if you're not sure what your gift is. Pray to God to reveal your gifts and trust in His timing. For many people, different talents emerge and develop over a lifetime of experiences. Your job is to approach all your endeavors with enthusiasm and an openness to try. Trying may be the first step needed for God to reveal the gifts He has blessed you with. God will join your special personality with the gifts and career He's planned for you.

# #45—Career Planning

# Big Plans

You've put in some heavy prayer time with God, and done some deep looking at yourself and your talents. You've explored different career avenues and discussed them with your parents. You're ready to look around. Take your time. There's a whole world out there. Explore and try a number of classes, summer jobs, and volunteer opportunities.

Okay, you've finally done it! Yes! You have, with prayer and God's direction, decided on a career goal! Career selection is often one of the most tense and confusing decisions in a person's life. But you and God worked through it together. You've made your career choice. Cool! Now what?

Career *planning* is the answer. Career planning is looking ahead and preparing to reach that career goal. There are personal, educational, and business achievements to meet before you can get into that career. Those achievements take both educational and financial planning. How do we get from Point A (choosing a career) to Point B (getting the job)? Get out your life map and check your location in God's plan. The answer is training—which you've already been saving for. There are a number of places to get it.

# The Education Equation

Getting an education is your choice. It's not your parent's, teacher's, or friend's choice. It's your choice because you have to *want* to learn. Up until now, you've been forced to go to school. It's the law. Career training is not law. You don't have to do it, but it will get you where you want to go. It's a simple equation—zero training equals zero chance of reaching those big career goals you've decided on.

Career education is the foundation for the rest of your life—whether you lay out DNA sequences or concrete for a living. Education can give you the basic tools to achieve God's plan for you. You can get this through on-the-job training, self training, college, or trade schools. (If you can work or study in a Christian environment, that would be great—but if not, make sure you have a network of spiritual support to help you deal with the non-Christian stuff.) Working hard is part of using your gifts and talents. You're God's witness on campus and at your job site. *"In the same way, let your light shine before men, that they may see your good deeds and praise your Father in heaven"* (Matthew 5:16).

# What Do You Get?

Education prepares you for your career by providing you with five things you'll need: knowledge, experience, connections, opportunities, and a competitive edge. This is true whether you go to university or trade school, or get on-the-job training.

(1) *Knowledge.* You need working knowledge—the know-how to apply what you learn and *do* the job. A surgeon has to apply his understanding of the human body to a real human body. Anyone want a surgeon who's not quite sure what to do?

(2) *Experience.* Part of any career education will include practical experience doing the work. Practice makes perfect. Practice the skills and procedures that make up your job. Animators draw hundreds of pictures before they graduate. Animation companies study the animator's college work before hiring her. Employers will hire the applicant with the best experience and references from former employers.

(3) *Connections.* Many of your instructors will have experience in the careers they teach about. They might be able to help you find summer work in the field or suggest companies that take volunteers. Employers hire individuals who have a history of making use of opportunities or who create opportunities for themselves. Ask your supervisors for letters of recommendation. These professionals might be able to help you get an interview. Top students or employees get noticed. Remember, connections work for you if you've already proven you know how to work hard.

Sometimes it doesn't seem like the odd jobs to save for your education, the study and endless classes, have any relationship to the real world. They do. Keep your head up. Concentrate on heading toward God's plan for you. It matches you perfectly. Enjoy every step of the way!

How you conduct yourself in the training field and in your education can be the reason you're hired or passed over. Remember, your work ethics are as important as your knowledge. Act like learning is your job. It is. Take your education plan seriously and work hard at it. Being diligent always pays off!

# #46—Getting a Job

# Hunt for the Right Employer

Working for the right employer can be even more important than getting a good job. You and your future boss are a team that should have the same business attitudes and values. To be enthusiastic in your job, you have to feel comfortable with the way things are done in that place of business (2 Corinthians 6:14). Consider each employer carefully, and pray. Have faith that God will help you find the right employer.

Getting to know a new employer is a process. Before you go to your job interview, find out all you can about that company. What is its business reputation? Is it a solid company with a promising future you can grow with? Does it have a good history with its employees? Learning all you can about your prospective employer is just as important as them learning about you.

# Resume

A resume is a written summary of your most important accomplishments. It shows your knowledge, experience, career connections, and competitive edge. It lets the employer know your value. Even your volunteer work counts. With your resume, send letters of recommendation from supervisors. Always remember, honesty in your resume is the most valuable thing there. Here are classic resume tips:

(1) *List your job experiences, education, and training.* Outline your main responsibilities and accomplishments.
(2) *Identify your strengths.* This is where your personality assessment shines.
(3) *Emphasize your accomplishments.* You were voted the employee of the month. Include things an employer might find interesting.
(4) *Put it together.* Put all these into a sharp, easy-to-read package. There are computer programs and books on resume style and format.
(5) *Stay focused.* Focus on what makes you shine. Don't make them guess at how best they can use your talents. Tell them why you're the right person for the job.

# The Interview

Okay, you landed an interview. The employer is naturally curious about you. Let his curiosity work for you. It's all in presentation. You have a short time in an interview to make an impression. Make it one of a hard worker who values a job opportunity. As soon as you enter the room, work to make the right presentation. Here are some close-up tips on how to get that close-up look.

(1) *Spend time in prayer before you go.* Ask God to give you the words, answers, wisdom, peace, and strength you need for the interview. Ask Him to help you get the job that's right for you.
(2) *Dress for success.* Wear what you would wear on the job or something you think relays the image you want.
(3) *Take care of the details.* Don't be late. Shake hands. Be friendly and confident. Don't fidget. Have good posture. Take a deep breath before you go into the meeting. Relax!
(4) *Be polite.* Introduce yourself. Speak calmly.
(5) *Balance your attitude.* Be thankful for the opportunity to be interviewed and let the interviewer know you would really like to work for his company. Balance your interviewer's view of you by presenting good past experience with a good future working attitude.

# Sigh!

You can breathe easy. The interview is over. Or is it? Always follow up an interview with a thank-you letter. Mail the letter that day to show your appreciation for the interview opportunity. A letter keeps your name fresh in the decision-maker's mind. When you get a job, thank both God and your future boss. Interviews—no sweat! Now get ready for the first day!

# No Callback

If you didn't get that callback, take it in stride. It doesn't mean you're no good, washed up, or a failure. It just means that you weren't right for that particular job. God's timing and direction play a big part here, too. Carry on to the next interview with just as much confidence. Most people go through several before they land that big job. Just trust that God will provide the job that's best for you.

# #47—Diligence

# Diligence: A Job Keeper

You got that job—how do you keep it? Through diligence. What is being diligent? It means giving special attention to the things that are expected of you. In other words, it is doing your job right and well. *"Diligent hands will rule, but laziness ends in slave labor"* (Proverbs 12:24). Diligence makes you valuable to the company.

(1) *Learn everything you can about your job.* The more you know about your job, the more valuable you will become. Knowledgeable employees are hard to replace.

(2) *Be responsible.* Be willing to take on more responsibilities. People who are willing to take charge and know when to step in get promotions.

(3) *Do what's right.* There are many times in our lives when we could cheat on our time card or do less than is expected without anybody noticing. When you work, who are you working for? God is really your main boss. *"Whatever you do, work at it with all your heart, as working for the Lord, not for men"* (Colossians 3:23). Do what you think is right and reveal your character.

(4) *Be an asset to your boss.* You don't have to jump through rings of fire to please your boss. Be punctual, cooperative, independent, enthusiastic, honest, and fun. If you do a good job and are easy to work with, that's valuable!

(5) *Work hard.* Whatever your job is, do it to the best of your abilities, from day one to your last day on the job.

(6) *Complete your tasks with speed and accuracy.* Don't be a time waster.

(7) *Don't let yourself be distracted by other things.* Take care of personal things on your own time, like during your breaks, not on work time.

(8) *Do your job and more.* Do those little extra things that make you stand out from others.

(9) *Always be on top of your profession.* Education is a lifelong process. Keep up with the trends.

# It's Time to Use Your Brain!

Way back in chapter two, we learned how some people worked harder and smarter to increase their value. That concept works for companies and individuals. Your career worth is partly determined by your employer's value of you. What can you bring to the company? Your employer knows your educational and business background. He met you and liked what he saw, but what else is there? You must prove to him that you will work hard for the company. You will use your time at work wisely and to the best of your ability. That doesn't mean working lots of overtime, it just means being efficient with your work and producing the most in the least amount of time. Your aim is to increase your productivity and your working knowledge of your job. Now, that's having a valuable attitude. Remember, every job you're given, from cleaning your room at home to being the president of a company, deserves the same work ethics. If you aren't ethical in one situation, you won't be in the other.

Work with your brain. Your "know-how" is your most important asset. An employee that can make a business system even better is an employee to keep. Take a tip from old Henry Ford by learning and applying new ways to old ideas. Working smarter increases your value to the company. *Do you see a man skilled in his work? He will serve before kings; he will not serve before obscure men*" (Proverbs 22:29). If you can make your company more valuable to your boss, other employees, and the community, you have shown your value. Being a hardworking and resourceful employee is being a solid Christian example in your workplace. *"His master replied, 'Well done, good and faithful servant! You have been faithful with a few things; I will put you in charge of many things. Come and share your master's happiness!'"* (Matthew 25:21). By far the most valuable thing you can bring to your job is a Christian example in your workplace.

# #48—Starting a Business

# The Big Boss

The boss is in control. He or she has authority to make decisions, decide who does each project, and how. Our personalities often determine whether we're bosses or employees. Both are important.

If you think you're the boss type, look into becoming an entrepreneur. They're the business adventurers. They pull a business together by joining idea with reality. It's risky. Entrepreneurs take the risk and thrive on the thrill. Many entrepreneurs are household names: Henry Ford, Thomas Edison, Alexander Bell, Mary Kay, Dave Thomas, Bill Gates. Entrepreneurialism is open to anybody. You just need the dream, knowledge, drive, and endurance to see it through. These people experienced failure before tasting success, but they didn't let it stop a lifetime dream.

# Getting in the Biz

Starting a business takes hours of thought, planning, and prayer. There are good and bad reasons to start your own business. Here are some good ones:

(1) You're convinced it's God's direction for you.
(2) You have a clear vision of the business you want to create and a passion to do it.
(3) You enjoy leadership and making important decisions: it suits your gifts and personality type.
(4) You have a personal drive to work and succeed—to "boldly go where no one has gone before."

Helping someone else succeed at business is a great way to prepare for running your own. The principles are the same. Pray, research, learn, and take each step carefully. Follow God's plan by saving for your business needs before you start your career. A year's worth of wages will help with your personal needs while your business is getting going. A good business leader knows how to use his own abilities and hire people to handle areas he's weak in. Know yourself and your business well before you open the doors.

# What Really Matters!

You've taken a journey to new and strange financial planets and explored the black holes of money matters. You've learned how to follow God's plan for your life, control the inside and outside you, give generously, conquer temptations, and work for your future by doing the right things today.

Money may have seemed important when you started the book, but is it really? It's part of a long string of inventions that have made our lives easier. Money's just a tool we use every day. How we handle money matters is about how we handle ourselves. What really matters? Our relationships with God, our families, and our community. That's what really matters!